GOD SO LOVED...

A student's guide to sharing Jesus at school

Second Edition

Lee Rogers
General Editor and Lead Author

missional
basics

Theme design by Robert Gurulé. Cover by Jiovan Garcia.

Chapter art by Mark Gettis, Jr. and Korinne Baker.

ISBN: 979-8-218-06735-9

Sermons and Small Group Lessons are available for download at
www.initiateconversations.com.

DEDICATION

For every Campus Missionary working to share Jesus at school and beyond, and for every youth leader coaching them along the way.

A Campus Missionary is a student who shares Jesus.

CONTENTS

To My Wife and Son
Thank you for the sacrifice of time and patience that allowed this vision
to become a reality. The late nights, early mornings, and lost weekends
will be redeemed as God's grace is proclaimed.

To The Contributing Authors
Thank you for believing in this book, and for giving your time, energy,
and experience to help students share Jesus with all who need to hear..

The stories told within these pages are real. The names of many of the participants have been changed for their privacy.

INTRODUCTION

Eight years ago God gave me a vision to create a tool that could help students have powerful conversations with their friends at school, and share Jesus in the process. At first I thought it would be something small, about the size of a credit card, with hints, shortcuts, and tricks to have conversations that connect to the Gospel. As I began to dive in to the concept of powerful conversations that lead to Jesus, I discovered there was much more to it than the amount of information that could fit onto a credit card.

It wasn't that a small and quick tool couldn't be designed, it was just that meaningful conversations require more than hints, shortcuts, and tricks. And at the end of the day, most people who make a lasting commitment to Jesus do so through a meaningful conversation with a friend.[1] So if we want people to make a lasting commitment to Jesus, we've got to learn how to have great conversations and how to be good friends. Let's do it right—let's not take shortcuts that short sell the Gospel.

The result of that vision was *Initiate: Powerful Conversations that Lead to Jesus*.[2] I wrote the book for middle and high school students, desiring to equip them to have conversations with their friends at school about Jesus. So I was surprised when youth pastors started telling me how helpful it was for them, and how they were taking their youth leaders through the book as a training tool. I was even more surprised when lead pastors started buying copies for their staff, using it as an instructional primer for having Spirit-led conversations with church members and visitors. I shouldn't have been surprised, because whether you're a teenager or elderly, the principles of great conversations are the same.

Not long after that, God gave me another vision to create a tool to help students have powerful conversations with their friends at school in order to share Jesus. The result of that vision was the first edition of this book. This is a different vision from *Initiate*, which was about having conversations that lead to Jesus in a very general way. *God So Loved: A*

1

Student's Guide to Sharing Jesus at School is about engaging the different groups of people in every student's life in order to share Jesus more effectively.

There are probably hundreds of people groups in any student's life, and this book covers a few: artists, athletes, family, religious groups, school clubs, hurting students, and many others. *God So Loved* explores the possibilities of serving each group of people by meeting their specific needs and having conversations based upon their uniqueness. This second edition of the book includes many people groups that have rose to prominence on campus and in student culture over the last six years, including transgender students, minority students, the backslidden, special needs students, and students who never feel good enough.

How To Use This Book

The first section of this book is titled "God So Loved the World," and is written to help students grasp the fullness of God's mission in their world, and how to share Jesus effectively by developing their testimony and communicating the Gospel. The second section of the book is titled "God So Loved My School," and it is the heart of the book. It contains 35 chapters, each written to help a Campus Missionary or Christian student share Jesus with a specific group of people in their school or life. Each chapter contains Scripture verses relevant to the people group, ideas for serving them, and questions to start a great conversation that leads to Jesus. The final section of the book looks forward (beyond high school) for the committed Christ-follower. There is also an appendix for homeschoolers, written by a homeschooler, to help them discover how to share Jesus in their own unique way.

God So Loved is the first book of its kind. It was born out of a vision God gave me, but it was accomplished by 30 authors representing the 35 people groups found in these pages. All of the authors have a passion for the Gospel, and a strong commitment to see Jesus shared on the school campus. I am thankful to each one of them for their time, energy, and thoughtfulness in preparing this book.

May God bless your efforts as you strive to share Jesus,

Lee Rogers, General Editor

---

[1] William Fay, *Share Jesus Without Fear* (Nashville: Broadman & Holman Publishers, 1999), 12.
[2] Available on Amazon.com.

GOD

SO

LOVED....

PART I
THE
WORLD

GOD
SO
LOVED....

HOW BIG IS THE WORLD?

Lee Rogers

I met my best friend when I was in college. We were both freshmen and living on the same floor, and for some reason we just clicked. Soon we were hanging out together, spending countless hours playing Madden '97 on his PlayStation (yes, the original PlayStation), and making late-night pizza runs. Dorm life was fun, and it cemented our friendship as we moved through this new stage of life together. It wasn't long before we became roommates.

A few people started calling us "The Prank Brothers," because we loved playing practical jokes around the dorm. One night around 2am we had a glow-in-the-dark hockey mask, and we quietly went from room to room, standing over the beds of our dorm mates, waiting for them to wake up to a glowing hockey mask hovering over them. More than one person jumped out of bed scared, or wildly kicked under the covers trying desperately to escape before they realized what was going on. Other times, when we were feeling less creative, we simply annoyed the rooms under us with the old "extension cord out the window" routine—hanging an extension cord out of the second story window to knock on the windows below. One way or another, we always managed to have a good time.

Soon we found more ways to have fun. We took road trips together, always adventuring and trying to make new memories. On one road trip we accidentally killed my parents' Chihuahua with fireworks. Don't worry—it didn't happen in the way you are picturing (it's a long story). Then there was the time my car caught on fire on the way to the car wash. Like a couple of college-aged geniuses, we figured the best way to put the fire out was to keep driving to the car wash and use the hose when we got there. My car died completely just 20 feet from the car wash bay, and we scrambled like a bunch of manic squirrels to find enough quarters to get the water turned on. Unfortunately the hose was too short to reach the car, but we still managed to "mist" the fire out from a distance. We were fine, but the car had to be towed.

Life moved forward and so did we. I got married, and my best friend became the best man in the wedding. Not long after, I served as the best man for his wedding. We had graduated from college, and started life in "the real world," but we still managed to find time to get together and have fun. 15 years later, we still get together on a regular basis to talk about life and everything that is going on.

I had a disturbing thought in the early years of our friendship. If we had met in high school, we wouldn't be best friends. In fact, we probably wouldn't be friends at all. We came into college as blank slates, not knowing anything about one another. But in high school, we would have known a lot more about one another. In particular, we would've known that we each ran in different social circles, circles that didn't intermingle much, if at all.

The High School Social Map

In high school I was into the arts; I was in plays, musicals, and chorus. I even did a short stint in the concert band, playing the timpani and the cymbals. My best friend from college was an athlete in high school. He was a corner back on the varsity football team, and he was good at it. We ran in different circles, had very different interests, and were looked at through different lenses by the high school population. We were on different locations of the High School Social Map.

It's not like this in every high school, but in my high school the arts didn't get a lot of attention. I went to a small rural high school and I had a pretty good experience there. But at the same time, I couldn't help but notice the way in which the athletes got most of the attention. It didn't really bother me that the athletic department got most of the school's extracurricular funding; more students in my high school were interested in athletics than the arts, so that is understandable.

It was more difficult to cope with the attitudes within the student body. There wasn't a lot of respect for the arts in my high school, especially among the athletes. There were a lot of sincerely nice athletes, but many of the others had no problem poking fun and looking down on students in the band, chorus, or any other student they didn't consider as being on their level. Even the Vo-Tech students weren't immune from their attitudes of superiority.

So in my high school athletes and artists didn't really intermingle. And while I could try to blame athletes for the situation, the full truth of the matter is that I was not interested in getting to know them either. I tended to lump all athletes into the same basket as the ones who used their status to bully others. As a Christian trying to share Jesus at school, I understood that God loved those athletes, and that He wanted them to put their faith in Christ, but I couldn't bring myself to start a conversation with them. My best friend and I wouldn't be friends at all if we had met in high school.

Here Be Dragons

It tends to be the same in all but the smallest of schools. Athletes and artists don't mix. Honors students and Vo-Tech students don't hang out together. Everyone seems to run around in his or her own circle, and no one tends to pay much attention to those outside the circle. In some ways, this is simply the way social life works. People like to hang out with people they have similar interests with. We all want to have friends with whom we share common ground, and it's likely we'll hang out with them most of the time. It's just natural. On this side of the map everyone is free to move within their own circle. It's safe and it's good.

But there is another side to this social map that isn't usually acknowledged, at least not in public. This side of the map is filled with insecurities and past hurts. It's labeled with warnings like "Do not enter," and "Here be dragons." On this side of the map, no one is free to move outside their own circle. It's dangerous and it's bad. The insecurities and past hurts that drive the labels on the map may not even be accurate or up to date, but it doesn't really matter. Why would anyone risk being eaten by a dragon?

This side of my map started to take shape when I was pretty young. I loved baseball, and I collected baseball cards every chance I got. I enrolled in Little League so I could start playing the sport I loved. I signed up, got a glove, got my uniform, and reported for practice. There was just one problem: I was terrible. And it didn't take long for my teammates to notice.

I was ridiculed for not being able to throw the ball hard enough, for striking out while the ball whizzed past me, and for not being able to catch a pop fly. If I was allowed off the bench to play a position, you were sure to find me in right field. But I didn't give up. I kept working at it. One game I caught a line drive out there in right field. Frankly, the ball was hit right into my glove, but it boosted my confidence and soon the fundamentals of the game seemed to come easier.

I actually started getting better. For the next three years I kept growing in my baseball skills. By the time I was moving into the 'major' division, I was one of the best players on my team. I was getting on base most of the time, and I was playing left and center field. I felt pretty good about it. Then something terrible happened...I moved up to middle school, and that meant moving up into the 'teener' league division.

The teener league meant playing on a bigger field with players who were older and better than I was. This wouldn't have been so bad, but something also happened to my game along the way. I lost the ability to judge the ball while in the outfield, and I was missing plays left and right. My batting suffered, too. Instead of getting on base most of the time, I was striking out most of the time.

I felt like I was back at the beginning, and so did my teammates. The same ridicule I had experienced as a boy was heaped on me again, but this time in teenage doses. I was on the wrong side of the map, surrounded by dragons ready to devour me. But now I was old enough to do something about it. I wasn't going to stick around trying to do something I wasn't good at just to be ridiculed and eaten by dragons. So I quit. I decided organized sports just weren't for me. I kept playing the 'backyard' version with my friends, but I was done trying to be an athlete. Instead, I focused on the things I was good at—the arts.

Dragons in the Mirror

Most people construct their own social map that includes an area of safety and good passage, and another, darker area where the dragons rule. We keep that mental map close at hand throughout middle school and high school. We have long memories, and we tend to not forget the times we were ridiculed by the dragons in our lives, or when we felt insecure because someone was better than us at something. And we decide the best and safest thing to do is not to roam close to dragon territory any longer. So we stay in our social circles, and we probably think the worst of the dragons.

The truth of the matter is, most dragons have their own social map too. And they don't consider themselves to be dragons. They consider themselves to be normal. They probably consider you to be a dragon. That's because they can't do the things you do, just like you can't do the things they do. So most of them don't stray outside of their social circles, and because they don't, they see you as a dragon. We are all somebody's dragon. Look in the mirror. You're looking at a dragon.

Go With a Globe

Not long after the earth was 'discovered' to be round in 1492, maps depicting the world as flat, and bearing the label "Here be dragons," went out of production. A round world required a round map, and that's when globes started to become popular. Seeing the world in a proper and accurate depiction changed the course of history. When it comes to our classmates in middle school and high school, we've also got to see them properly and accurately. They aren't dragons. Dragons aren't real. Instead, we must see them as God sees them: individuals in need of salvation.

John 3:16 says, "For *God so loved the world* that he gave his one and only Son, that whoever believes in him shall not perish but have eternal life."[1] This is the most inclusive type of love possible. It is impossible for anyone to be outside of this love. God so loved the world means God so loved everyone. That's why the verse also says, "whoever believes in him shall not perish but have eternal life." The only qualification for eternal life is belief. Anyone who believes experiences salvation. This is a global love from a global God; a map cannot contain this love. The world is round. The world is not flat. And there is no such thing as dragons.

God so loved football players and band members. God so loved Vo-Tech students and Student Leaders. God so loved nerds and cheerleaders. God so loved quiet students and vocalists. God so loved soccer players and honors students. God so loved loners and theatre students. God so loved atheists and believers. God so loved every single person you encounter every single day. And it's time to start acting like it. It's time to stop viewing school as a social map, and start viewing your classmates with a global love. Lay your insecurities and past hurts at the foot of the cross, and start loving and serving everyone you see at school, no matter how different they are from you.

God's Church and Your School

One of the most well-known verses of the New Testament speaks to the openness and diversity of the early church. Galatians 3:28 says, "There is neither Jew nor Greek, there is neither slave nor free, there is no male and female, for you are all one in Christ Jesus."[2] There was no room in God's church for social prejudices or fearful biases. Anyone who believed in Jesus was welcome. The cross of Jesus Christ makes everyone the same, and the early church knew this better than many of us do today.

For the early church, Galatians 3:28 wasn't simply empty words. They embraced a global love of God, recognizing that God's love wasn't just for people like the disciples, but that it was for everyone. Acts 13:1 lists the names and descriptions of the leaders of the early church at Antioch in Syria. It reveals a diverse group of individuals coming together in the name of Jesus. Here's the role call:

- Barnabas, who was born on the island of Cyprus in the Mediterranean and descended from the priestly tribe of the Jews.
- Simeon who was called Niger. Niger is latin for black, and this nickname is meant to show that he had a darker complexion than most Syrians; he probably came from North Africa.[3]
- Lucius of Cyrene, from the North African coast, whose name indicates he was raised as a Roman.[4]
- Manaen, who was from the upper classes of society, raised in a royal court alongside one of the rulers of the region.[5]
- Saul, also known as Paul, was both a Roman citizen and a Jew, in addition to being extremely well educated. He had been an enemy of the early church, overseeing the murder of Stephen before Christ appeared to him on the Damascus Road.

The leaders of the church in Antioch were about as diverse a group as one could find during that time. They came from different levels of social status, different religious backgrounds, different cultures, and they had even been enemies at one time. But they all recognized their equality at the foot of the cross. They accepted one another, just as Christ had accepted them. If the early church were made up of students from your high school, the role call may have read like this:

- Tom, the football player who is nice to everyone.
- Michael, the underprivileged student studying auto mechanics at Vo-Tech.
- Lydia, the honors student with a scholarship to Harvard.
- Christopher, who was born to millionaires and grew up in a mansion.
- Andrew, who used to have an anger problem and hated everyone, bullying them with his size.

God's church is made up of people from all different walks of life, interests, and backgrounds. He didn't send Jesus to die so that heaven could be filled with people just like you. He sent Jesus to die so that *anyone* who believed in Him could receive salvation, no matter how different they are from you. So whether you play sports or are into the arts, whether you are bound for an Ivy League school after graduation or headed into the workforce, we are all equal at the cross of Christ. And we must share Jesus with *everyone* in our school.

How Big is Your World?

God so loved the *world*. How big is your concept of the world? Most Christian teenagers I know would rather go around the world on a missions trip to share Jesus with a child in Africa than walk across a classroom in their high school and start a conversation about God with someone different from themselves. You may travel around the world, but if that observation describes you, your world is much smaller than you think. How big is your world?

How big is God's love? If your idea of God's love isn't big enough to include every single person in your high school, then your concept of God's love isn't big enough. More importantly, if your attitude and behavior towards every single person in your school doesn't include the possibility of serving them, getting to know them better, and starting conversations that lead to Jesus, then your concept of God's love is too small. God so loved the *world*. God so loved *your world*. God so loved *your school*.

This book is designed to help you serve and start conversations with all different kinds of people in your middle school or high school. It doesn't include every single type of person, and not every single person in your school will fit into the molds that have been developed in these pages. Even so, this book will equip you to share Jesus in the world of your school with ideas and conversation starters that can't be found anywhere else. Every person in your school needs to hear about Jesus so that they may make their own decision about who He is, and whether or not they will follow Him.

---

[1] NIV

[2] ESV.

[3] Clinton E. Arnold, "Acts," in *John, Acts*, vol. 2 of *Zondervan Illustrated Bible Backgrounds Commentary: New Testament*, Accordance electronic ed. (Grand Rapids: Zondervan, 2002), 333.

[4] F. F. Bruce, *The Book of the Acts*, New International Commentary on the New Testament. Accordance electronic ed. (Grand Rapids: Eerdmans, 1988), 245.

[5] Craig S. Keener, *The IVP Bible Background Commentary: New Testament*, Accordance electronic ed. (Downers Grove: InterVarsity Press, 1993), 357.

GOD
SO
LOVED....

2
ME
Lee Rogers & Kent Hulbert

A few years ago, I was coaching a Bible club at a large high school in the town where I was a youth pastor. The club was discussing different ways to share Jesus with their school. Like many Bible clubs, this club was filled with students from many different Christian traditions—Baptists, Alliance Students, Catholics, Methodists, Assemblies of God, and a few others. Each of these churches, and the students representing them in the Bible club, had their own ideas and teachings of the best way to share Jesus and spread the Gospel. From time to time, those different viewpoints can create tension between believers, and today was no different.

Many of the students presented fantastic ideas; giving the sports teams water bottles with Scripture on them, placing encouraging 'post-it' notes in the girls' bathrooms telling them they are beautifully created in God's image, and having a 'Battle of the Bands' with a guest speaker to share the Gospel between the bands. As a youth pastor, I was thrilled at the ideas being shared. However, the President of the Bible Club was nervous, and soon expressed why.

She said, "I always think the best way to share Jesus is to live our lives as a good example, so that people will see what's different about us and decide to follow Jesus." She went on to explain that she wasn't very comfortable with the idea of actually telling people about Jesus, and she'd rather the Club just find ways to be nice and spread good cheer throughout the school. She was concerned that talking about Jesus would offend people, and believed that if she could just be nice, everyone would like her and soon follow Christ.

It was a safe course of action with only one problem: no one will ever hear about Jesus through good deeds or kindness alone, because good deeds and kindness do not have a voice. Only people have voices, and while doing something kind may open a door for you to share Jesus, the kind deed in itself can't lead anyone to Christ. You will eventually have to open your mouth and talk about God, talk about *why* you are being so nice and kind, in order for people to know about Him.

The Necessity of Words

The Bible Club president had fallen into a trap in her thinking that is all too common today; the belief that if Christians can just be nice enough, everyone will want to be like us. And being nice means *not* telling people about Jesus, because Jesus is offensive to some. I've fallen into that trap myself in the past, praying, "God, let them see a difference in me, and turn to you as a result." This kind of thinking has two primary problems; the first is that it is unbiblical, and the second is that it doesn't work. It is always necessary to use words to tell people about Jesus, if they are ever going to become Christians.

The Apostle Paul used simple logic in making this case in Romans 10. He wrote:

> *"Everyone who calls on the name of the Lord will be saved. How, then, can they call on the one they have not believed in? And how can they believe in the one of whom they have not heard? And how can they hear without someone preaching to them?"*[1]

Read that Scripture passage again, because I don't want you to miss it. Did you catch it? *How can they hear without someone preaching to them?* Here's the Apostles Paul's flow of thought if you take it in reverse:

Preaching ➜ Hearing ➜ Belief ➜ Calling ➜ Salvation

It's really quite simple. No one hears about Jesus unless someone opens up his or her mouth and declares that He is Lord. Preaching leads to hearing, hearing leads to belief, belief leads to calling upon the Lord, and calling upon the Lord leads to salvation.

There are some who would claim that being kind is a type of preaching, and that doing good deeds proclaims Jesus is Lord just as much as opening your mouth. This is a very nice thought that is entirely incorrect. The Apostle Paul wrote this in the Greek language, and used a word that is unmistakable to describe what he meant, the word *kērussō*. It

18

means "*to proclaim after the manner of a herald*; always with a suggestion of formality, gravity, and an authority which must be listened to and obeyed."[2] In other words, Paul wasn't just saying to share the Gospel, but to proclaim it like a royal edict in the public square, with power and authority. It can be written and published, or spoken and preached, but one way or another the Gospel must be shared through the use of words. To believe or behave otherwise is unbiblical.

The second reason we can't *only* be nice is that it doesn't work. You can be a nice Christian, and you should be a nice Christian, but your niceness won't compel anyone to ask why you are so nice. The truth is there are nice people in nearly every religion. There are nice Jews, Muslims, Buddhists, and even Atheists. Hindus value hospitality as a point of their religious practice; they are oftentimes more kind than Christians. Even though you should always be as kind and as generous as possible, those actions alone are not enough to distinguish Christianity from any other religion, let alone lead anyone to Christ. It's only when you combine good deeds with proclaiming the Gospel verbally that anyone can come to faith in Christ. That's why the Apostle Paul wrote, "So faith comes from hearing, and hearing by the word of Christ."[3] He did *not* write, "Faith comes from seeing, seeing your good deeds."

Developing Your Story[4]

Having to share Jesus by opening our mouths and talking about Him can seem intimidating, but it doesn't have to be that way. That's because explaining how *God So Loved* your friend begins by explaining how *God So Loved* you. Most people are very comfortable talking about themselves, and sharing Jesus involves talking about yourself, telling your story. It is the story of how God has changed your life, given you hope, or any other way in which grace has been made evident to you. These stories are powerful, and can help your friend receive the Gospel because they see it at work in you!

A lot of people may have a difficult time believing the Bible, or accepting the word of the church or a preacher. But most people will respect your personal stories, feelings, and experiences. Stories are real. Stories are memorable. Stories leave an impression of personal truth. Your story tells others about God's power at work in your life. It's not an explanation of how Jesus saves us, or even a plea for salvation. But it does demonstrate an experience of God in your life—a God-story! A God-story is a personal truth that cannot be taken away from you. Have you ever felt a great sense of peace from God? That's a God-story! Have you been healed, or has someone in your family been healed? That's a God-story! Do you turn to God in prayer when you're worried about something? That's a God-story!

Your story is the testimony of how God touched your life. But it can also be smaller stories of how God has worked in you or around you. Your testimony of God's work in your life is powerful. In Revelation 12, a story is told about a war in heaven between the angels and Satan, who is called the "accuser of the brethren." We are the brethren. Verse 11 says Satan was conquered "by the blood of the Lamb, and the word of their (the brethren's) testimony." The two most powerful things in Satan's ultimate defeat are (1) the Blood of the Lamb—Jesus sacrifice on the cross, and (2) the word of our testimony—when we share what God has done for us. This is simply amazing! Did you know there was so much power in your story?

Shaping your testimony is easier than you think. In his book, *The Coffeehouse Gospel*, Matthew Paul Turner offers the following questions to help you discover your own story:[5]

1. What was your childhood like? Were you a churchgoer? Was a life in Jesus something you pursued? If not, did you believe in anything remotely spiritual?
2. When was the first time you remember hearing about God, Jesus, or the Christian faith? How old were you?
3. What was your immediate response to the Gospel?
4. If you grew up knowing Jesus, was there a time that you remember it really clicking? Can you explain this turn of events?
5. If you resisted your first hearing of the Gospel message, what is the main reason you didn't believe at first?
6. What ultimately changed your heart toward the Gospel message?
7. Were there any life occurrences—a death in the family, illness, a miracle, a new relationship, etc.—that stood out as landmarks to you on your journey of faith?
8. How did God use these life landmarks to pull you into a relationship with Him?
9. What attracted you to know more about Jesus? What part of your relationship with Him has influenced you the most?
10. What about your life changed after you made your decision to be a Jesus follower?

Answer these questions thoughtfully, then begin to write out your story.

It's not necessary for you to always share your full testimony, however. In fact, often it's more natural just to share one brief story about how God worked in your life. This is a God-story. William Peel and Walt Larimore give a few tips for developing your own stories about your faith in God, and how they've impacted your life. They write:[6]

- Make a list of the times when you had a meaningful encounter with God. It may have been a time:
  o When God did something meaningful or significant in your life
  o When you enjoyed and experienced pleasure in your relationship with God
  o When you experienced intimacy or renewal in your relationship with God
  o When God spoke clearly to you or gave you guidance
  o When God worked through you to accomplish His purposes
- Choose one or two of these experiences and write a brief faith story about each

When you've got some God-stories down, practice them! Ask a Christian friend if you can share them. Ask your pastor if you can give your testimony or story in church or youth group. Above all else, look for opportunities to share your story as you listen to the stories of others. Don't force it! Wait for the invitation from your friend or a nudging from the Holy Spirit. Your story can open up the door for you to explain the Gospel.

Explaining the Gospel

God So Loved IS the greatest message of love, redemption, justice, and hope that every person must know. It would be disingenuous for a book to provide ways to start a conversation to share Christ's hope without also providing a way to communicate that hope clearly. Below is a method to share the Gospel—that God so loved—so others can understand and know this love for themselves. It's called *Alive in Five*, and it's designed for you to sit down with a friend and explain the message and ask discussion questions as you effectively communicate the Gospel.[7] Remember to share your testimony along the way as you share. Illustrate the message of the Gospel by sharing how it worked in your own life.

God is love.

God is the definition of love, and He loves us deeply. God's love for us is reliable, everlasting, and has no limits! And there is nothing we can do to earn His love; it is given to us freely. God still loves us when we do wrong, or when we feel shame. God loves us even when we reject Him or if we deny His existence! God not only loves you, but He also loves the entire world—every person in every culture and religion! God's love is the most inclusive love in the universe. No one can escape His love.

It's like this...

God created everything, and even the simple things He created are examples of how He loves us. God has given us air to breathe and water to drink. He's given us the sun to keep us warm and give us light. God has given us every simple thing, because God thinks about us! As Max Lucado wrote, "If God had a refrigerator, your picture would be on it!"

Bible Verses:

1 John 4:16, "We know how much God loves us, and we have put our trust in his love. God is love, and all who live in love live in God, and God lives in them."

Psalms 86:15, "But you, O Lord, are a God of compassion and mercy, slow to get angry and filled with unfailing love and faithfulness."

1 John 4:7-8, "Dear friends, let us continue to love one another, for love comes from God. Anyone who loves is a child of God and knows God. But anyone who does not love does not know God, for God is love."

More Bible verses to read: Psalm 139, Jeremiah 29:11, John 3:16, Romans 8:38-39, 1 Corinthians 13:4-8, Ephesians 2:4-5.

Think about it...

In what ways have you experienced love?

In what ways have you seen or felt God's love?

Our sin divides us from God.

Sin is a problem every person has—a problem we all share. Sin happens when we miss the target of perfect love—God's love. Sin is disobedience to God and includes both wrongful actions and even certain thoughts. It includes lawlessness, hateful behavior, violence, and failing to do what is right. Sin creates division between our friends and us, and between God and us. We as humans have a tendency or bias to commit sin. We begin life, and before long, start going our own way rather than following God's way because of sin. All the problems of the human race, big and small, come from sin. Our sin doesn't stop God from loving us; however, when we sin, we move away from God and create distance between us.

It's like this…
Imagine an archer who draws back his bow and sends an arrow toward a target, but instead of hitting the bull's-eye, the arrow veers off course and misses the mark. The arrow may miss by a little or by a lot - but the result is the same: the arrow doesn't land where it's supposed to. The same is true of sin—we miss the mark.

Bible Verses:
1 John 3:4, "Everyone who sins is breaking God's law, for all sin is contrary to the law of God."

Isaiah 59:2, "It's your sins that have cut you off from God. Because of your sins, he has turned away and will not listen anymore."

More Bible verse to read: Psalm 66:18, Luke 15:11-32, Romans 3:10-12, Galatians 5:4, Ephesians 2:12.

Think about it…
In what ways has sin created division between you and others?

In what ways has sin separated you from God?

Jesus died for our sin, then came back to life.

Although our sin divides us from God, the separation is not the end of the story. While we were separated because of sin, God's showed his perfect love by sending Jesus, His Son, to live a sinless life and die a sacrificial death for us. God's perfect love resulted in the perfect action to pay for our sin: He erased it and reconnected us to Himself. Not only did Jesus demonstrate God's perfect love by dying, He also demonstrated His perfect power by conquering death and coming back to life. Through His death and new life, we also have hope for a new life!

It's like this...

When a crime is committed, society demands that justice be done. The criminal has to pay the price for his or her wrong action; usually by going to jail and/ or repaying the victims. Jesus paid the price for all sins of humanity, all the sin—past, present, future—for all of time. He not only paid the price, he also came back to life victoriously!

Bible Verses:

Romans 5:8, "But God showed his great love for us by sending Christ to die for us while we were still sinners."

1 Peter 3:18, "Christ suffered for our sins once for all time. He never sinned, but he died for sinners to bring you safely home to God. He suffered physical death, but he was raised to life in the Spirit."

Romans 6:9-10, "We are sure of this because Christ was raised from the dead, and he will never die again. Death no longer has any power over him. When he died, he died once to break the power of sin. But now that he lives, he lives for the glory of God."

More Bible verses to read: Matthew 28:6, Luke 24:46-47, John 3:16, 1 Corinthians 15:3-4, 2 Corinthians 5:21, Titus 3:5-7.

Think about it...

Think of a time you did wrong and had to be punished or pay a price. What did that feel like?

What would it have felt like if someone were to take the punishment and pay the price for you?

We need to decide to put our faith in God.

God's perfect love accomplished perfect justice through Jesus, yet that same love also gives us a choice to have faith in God or not. Faith is our belief, our firm conviction, of things we do not see. God does not force belief upon us; His love allows us to make the decision. Jesus paid the price to save us from our sin, but to receive that salvation we must put our faith in God. We do that by making Jesus our Lord and believing that God raised Him from the dead. When we put our trust in God, we have faith. Our faith enables us to receive God's grace.

It's like this...
Have you ever been given a gift card? We receive gift cards as gifts, but unless you use them, they are just plastic. You must act on the gift card offer. In the same way, our faith in God makes Jesus' death, resurrection, and the forgiveness of sin effective in our lives. You must act on God's offer.

Bible Verses:
John 3:16, "For this is how God loved the world: He gave his one and only Son, so that everyone who believes in him will not perish but have eternal life."

Hebrews 11:6, "And it is impossible to please God without faith. Anyone who wants to come to him must believe that God exists and that he rewards those who sincerely seek him."

Romans 10:9-10, "If you openly declare that Jesus is Lord and believe in your heart that God raised him from the dead, you will be saved. For it is by believing in your heart that you are made right with God, and it is by openly declaring your faith that you are saved."

More Bible verses to read: Romans 10:13, 2 Corinthians 5:17, Ephesians 2:8, Titus 2:11, Hebrews 11:1.

Think about it...
What are some things you believe exist even though you can't see them? For example: the wind, the love of our parents or friends, etc.

What is preventing you from having faith in God, and in Jesus' death and resurrection?

The Holy Spirit will help us live for God.

Jesus died for our sin, but He also died so that we could have a better life by living a selfless life—a life focused on God and His perfect love. It's hard to live unselfishly, but God sent the Holy Spirit to help us! Like Jesus, the Holy Spirit is God. The Holy Spirit teaches us and gives us passion for God. The Holy Spirit also gives us power to be who God wants us to be and to do what God wants us to do. We can hear from the Holy Spirit through prayer and reading God's Word—the Bible. The power of the Holy Spirit is most often experienced in gatherings with other followers of Christ—the Church.

It's like this...
When Jesus' disciples had their first encounter with the Holy Spirit, two key words were used to describe it—wind and fire. The Holy Spirit is like a powerful wind— we feel even though we do not see. A powerful wind can usher in change and move things around. In the same way, the Holy Spirit can move us and bring change to our lives or our situations. The Holy Spirit is also like fire—purifying us, exciting us, and drawing us closer to God.

Bible Verses:
2 Corinthians 5:15, "He died for everyone so that those who receive his new life will no longer live for themselves. Instead, they will live for Christ, who died and was raised for them."

John 14:26, "But when the Father sends the Advocate as my representative—that is, the Holy Spirit—he will teach you everything and will remind you of everything I have told you."

Acts 1:8, "But you will receive power when the Holy Spirit comes upon you. And you will be my witnesses, telling people about me everywhere—in Jerusalem, throughout Judea, in Samaria, and to the ends of the earth."

Think about it...
In what ways do you need the Holy Spirit to help you live for God?

What church or gathering of believers can you be a part of so that you may experience the power of the Holy Spirit?

Close With The Point

When you share the Gospel, it is important that the person you are sharing with responds to what you have shared. Close your conversation with this truth: You can't just hear or read about the Gospel for it to be effective in your life—you must believe it! It's similar to a winning code on your favorite soft-drink bottle or candy bar wrapper; the winning code doesn't have any value unless you redeem it. To accept Christ's Gospel offer requires a response. Ask if they are ready to accept it. It's simple, "Are you ready to accept Christ's free gift offered to anyone who puts their trust in Him?"

If they hesitate, ask if there is anything holding them back. Let them know they can start this new relationship with God now! Why wait? Share that they can begin to place their trust in Jesus alone through a prayer. It's not the prayer that saves them, it's the heart behind it: placing their soul and life in Jesus alone. Re-lead them thru the GOSPEL as you pray together. You might say something like:

"Dear God,

I believe that you are real, that you love me, and that I have been separated from you by sin.

I know that I cannot save myself from sin. I know that only you can save me.

Thank you for sending Jesus to pay the price for my sin.

I believe that Jesus is Lord, that He paid the price for my sin with His death, and that you raised Him from the dead.

Please forgive me as I accept you into my life and help me through Your Holy Spirit.

Help me to live for you.

Amen.."[8]

Next Steps

Celebrate with your friend! Encourage your friend—this is just the beginning for this new relationship with God! Help your friend get plugged in to a church where they can grow with God and with other believers. Help your friend to learn how to pray and read the Bible. Connect your friend to a youth pastor or leader who could become a spiritual mentor to him or her. Consider getting the *Alive in Christ* booklet for your friend. This booklet is designed to help your friend through his or her first few weeks of faith. It's available for a low cost at www.myhealthychurch.com. Encourage your friend to tell someone else about Jesus and how God So Loved!

---

[1] Romans 10:13–14 NIV

[2] *Thayer's Greek-English Lexicon of the New Testament,* "κηρύσσω," Accordance electronic edition.

[3] Romans 10:17 NASB

[4] Portions of this section are taken from Chapter 6 of *Initiate: Powerful Conversations That Lead to Jesus* (Createspace: 2014).

[5] Matthew Paul Turner, *The Coffeehouse Gospel: Sharing Your Faith in Everyday Conversation* (Lake Mary, FL: Relevant Books, 2004), 96-97.

[6] William Carr Peel and Walt Larimore, *Going Public with Your Faith* (Grand Rapids: Zondervan, 2003), 96.

[7] *Alive in Five* is available at www.myhealthychurch.com. *Alive in Five* is © 2019 by Sulubris Resources, 1445 N. Boonville Ave., Springfield, MO 65802. Used by permission. All scriptures in the *Alive in Five* section are from the New Living Translation.

[8] This sample prayer is from *Alive in Five.*

GOD

SO

LOVED....

PART II
MY
SCHOOL

GOD
SO
LOVED...

3

BAND STUDENTS

Doug Sayers

Being involved in the band was not my first idea. You see, I had a love for football, but what's a guy 5' tall and just over 100 lbs. going to do on the field except land up in the hospital with missing limbs and a victim of the concussion protocol? Or worse, go through twice-a-day practices only to stand on the sidelines chatting it up with the water boy. Nope...not gonna happen! So I thought it through—if I joined the band, I could still have a network of friends at school and still get into all the games, home or away, for free. What a great idea! So I did it, I joined the band.

Band was not as easy as I first thought it would be. Not owning an instrument of my own, I was told I would be given the school's most prestigious instrument. It also turned out to be their largest and heaviest instrument—the brass tuba! Then there were the 90° and 90% humidity days spent at band camp. We memorized the music, marched on the field, and learned the show with lots of steps, patterns, counting, and cadences. Next there was the band uniform: hats with plumes, pants with adjustable clips so they could fit someone with a waist size anywhere from 20-40 inches, and a jacket proudly sporting our school colors of blue and white along with our mascot, an eagle.

Oh, I almost forgot—we also had to buy bucks. What? You don't know what bucks are??? Neither did I! Soon I learned they were white shoes with black soles. They had to be polished for inspection before every game, parade, and pep rally. Yes, unlike the football team, our band uniforms had all the stylings of decades long gone. So much for free football.

Being part of the band was like being part of a military unit going into a great battle with the hope of a victory to bring home to the rest of the school. It was a rowdy time with lots of energy, chants and cheers all in an effort to defend the honor of our school by adding a check in the win column.

Though the football team is often the centerpiece of the battle. It is the band that:

- Signals the start of the game
- Announces each touchdown and field goal scored
- Owns the field for the half time show
- Is last to be heard announcing the win

Musicians have always been a part of the battle. Joshua 6 describes the battle of Jericho and the musicians played a major role. Jericho was a wicked city that stood between the army of Israel and the land that God had promised them. The battle plan was not drawn up by man, but was delivered to Joshua by God himself. Pay attention to the importance that God placed upon the musicians:

> *Now the gates of Jericho were securely barred because of the Israelites. No one went out and no one came in.*

> *Then the LORD said to Joshua, "See, I have delivered Jericho into your hands, along with its king and its fighting men. March around the city once with all the armed men. Do this for six days. Have seven priests carry trumpets of rams' horns in front of the ark. On the seventh day, march around the city seven times, with the priests blowing the trumpets. When you hear them sound a long blast on the trumpets, have the whole army give a loud shout; then the wall of the city will collapse and the army will go up, everyone straight in.*
> Joshua 6:1-5 NIV

There is reason to love band members, to love musicians: God does not put the focus on the fighting men but on His musicians. It is the musicians that:

- Lead the fighting men into battle.
- Sound the blast on the trumpets signaling the whole army to shout!

- Lead the shout of God that brings the walls down so the fighting men can then clean up!

God loves the musician and has filled the heavens and earth with music. Here's what happened in Jericho:

> *On the seventh day, they got up at daybreak and marched around*
> *the city seven times in the same manner, except that on that day*
> *they circled the city seven times. The seventh time around, when the*
> *priests sounded the trumpet blast, Joshua commanded the army,*
> *"Shout! For the LORD has given you the city!"*
>
> *When the trumpets sounded, the army shouted, and at the sound*
> *of the trumpet, when the men gave a loud shout, the wall collapsed;*
> *so everyone charged straight in, and they took the city.*
> Joshua 6:15-16, 20 NIV

Being a musician is the coolest thing in the world. God so loved music and musicians, and we must love them too. Furthermore, just like anyone else, musicians need Jesus.

If we really want to share Jesus with musicians, we must demonstrate Jesus' love to them. Jesus went about doing good[1], and so should we. So how can we serve band members?

Clean and Polish

It's amazing how muddy a well-played football field can become. This mud often ends up on instruments. I will tell you that even though band members are told to clean the instruments, they all HATE to do it! You can serve by offering to help clean instruments. It's important to be taught how to clean instruments before you try it alone. There are many delicate parts that can be damaged by a well-intentioned, but ill-equipped friend. It's always better to do this together which also continues to build your relationship.

Clean and Polish Again

It's not only the instruments that get muddy; the shoes really take a beating. Remember me telling you that we had to polish our shoes for inspection on a regular basis? You can very practically demonstrate what Christ-like humility is by cleaning and polishing your friend's marching band shoes. Jesus literally washed the feet of his disciples, and we should be doing the same. In our culture, this is about as close to a literal foot washing as you can get without being awkward. This takes less skill than cleaning instruments, but you will be a hero to band members for taking on this task and doing it well.

Have a Blast—Confetti Cannons

Confetti cannons can be a blast for the marching band! They make an awesome visual display after each touchdown, and they are just fun to use! Confetti cannons are available at party stores, and you can even get them at Walmart. Your friends in the band won't soon forget you for giving them this much fun!

Great Food, Hot Chocolate

Football games and band competitions often take place in colder weather, and band members are freezing in the stands. Make arrangements with the band director to bring cookies, brownies, and hot chocolate. Ask when the best time to serve them will be. Put a couple of chocolate chip cookies in a baggie to pass out and share. You may even put an encouraging scripture verse tied to the cookies. Another idea for cold weather is to pass out inexpensive hand warmers. But cold weather or not—band members love food!

Pray Together

If you develop a close relationship with a fellow band member, invite them to pray with you before taking the field. Pray for a great performance, for everyone to play their best, and for the favor of the audience. Pray specifically for your friend—that they would play better than ever before. Even if they're not a believer, you can still ask, "Would you mind praying with me? I like to pray, but I like praying with someone else best." After the show, thank them for praying with you.

Having a Conversation

Most musicians love to talk although some may be more quiet than others.[2] Most musicians have their interest in music, musical styles, and their favorite musicians in common. There is almost an endless list of questions that you, as a Campus Missionary/Christian, can ask a musician that will lead to meaningful conversations about Jesus.

- **What got you started in music? What's your journey been like?** Show an interest in their life. When they start sharing, you'll learn a lot about their personal history. Many musicians have some connection to the church. When it's your turn to share your story, be sure to connect it to God.

- **Do you play in any other bands? What is that like?** This is where you begin to hear about their music interest outside of school. You may have an opportunity to talk about your youth ministry band. When your relationship progresses enough, you might even be able to invite them to join your youth group or church worship band or orchestra.

- **Do you play any other instruments? What is your favorite instrument to play? What makes it your favorite?** Many musicians play more than one instrument. The one that you have seen them play may not actually be their primary instrument.

- **Do you think music will be a part of your future? If you could do anything with your musical ability, what would it be?** Often musicians dream of being the next platinum record holder or of making a career out of music in some way. Help uncover those dreams with these questions. Dreams give hope, and you have an opportunity to develop this hope in their lives. Jeremiah 29:11 says, "For I know the plans I have for you, declares the Lord, plans to prosper you and not harm you, plans to give you hope and a future." What role could God be playing in inspiring these dreams? What are your dreams? Are you prepared to share them?

- Share the story of Jericho and the musicians. Then ask, **"What made music so powerful in this story? What do you think God knows about music? What does He think about musicians?"** Even if your friend doesn't believe in God, it's still an interesting story that's been proven historically true by archeologists.[3] This will make for a great discussion, and as with any discussion, you'll have the opportunity to share your point of view.

---

[1] Acts 10:38.

[2] See the chapter on "Quiet Students".

[3] For a thorough and detailed archeological analysis of Jericho, check out the article "Did the Israelites Conquer Jericho? A New Look at the Archeological Evidence" by Bryant G. Wood, PhD, on www.biblearcheology.org.

GOD
SO
LOVED....

<u>4</u>

THEATRE STUDENTS

Sam Blevins

"All the world's a stage,
and all the men and women merely players."
William Shakespeare

Everybody loves a good story. Much of our everyday conversations consist of storytelling. It's how we share our experiences and connect with others in a way that we can relate to. However, I would be willing to bet that not many appreciate stories as much as theatre students do! They memorize countless amounts of lines, endure long, sweaty rehearsals, and give up their evenings and free time for the purpose of telling a story worth telling. Sadly, many theatre students are waiting to hear the greatest story of all: God's story.

God loves drama. Just take a look at the Bible! There are epic battles of impossible odds that put "The Battle of Helm's Deep" from *Lord of the Rings: The Two Towers* to shame. Forget about *The Notebook*, have you read Hosea? How about when Joshua sent two spies to infiltrate Jericho like something out of a *Mission Impossible* movie? However, all of these stories are simply subplots for God's greatest story: His redemption of all mankind. We were fallen and helpless. Mankind had rebelled against God and turned from His ways. Even our best attempts fell pathetically short of God's standards. All hope was lost, but then God stepped in and changed everything.

The law of Moses was unable to save us
because of the weakness of our sinful nature.
So God did what the law could not do. He sent
his own Son in a body like the bodies we
winners have. And in that body God declared

39

an end to sin's control over us by giving his Son
as a sacrifice for our sins. He did this so that
the just requirement of the law would be fully
satisfied for us, who no longer follow our sinful
nature but instead follow the Spirit.
Romans 8:3-4 NLT

God won the ultimate victory. He loved us so much that He would send his own Son to take the punishment that we should have had. He paid the ultimate price so that we could be together. How incredible is that? But wait, there's more! Not only are we forgiven of our sins, but God also wants to change, transform, and equip us to be the fullness of what He created us to be. When we commit our lives to Him, He is working in our lives to make us the best possible versions of ourselves. We are God's masterpiece. Every person you have ever met is a unique glimpse into the beauty of God, because we are created in his image. God's story didn't end with the Bible; it is being continued in your life!

Theatre was a big part of my high school and college years. My high school was doing a production of *Into the Woods*, a musical comedy about fairy tales, and they needed more singers. I was heavily involved in the music classes, so I decided that it might be fun to try out for it. I got the part of Rapunzel's Prince, and was thrilled at the opportunity to sing and perform on stage. Rehearsals began, and we spent every evening for months learning the music, our lines, entrances, exits, and blocking. All of these things are important, and vital to learn for a play to be successful, but the part of being in a play that I loved most and kept me doing plays was how well you got to know people.

Throughout those months, I got to know everyone involved in the play very well. Many of us would often stand in the parking lot after rehearsal ended for another hour or two talking, or we would go grab dinner at a fast food restaurant before heading home. Most of the conversations were light hearted, with topics such as difficult classes we were taking, movies or video games that were coming out, and music. Other times God would open up opportunities to talk about deeper things, and I would be in the position to share encouragement because of the friendship we had built.

After our final performance of *Into the Woods*, I realized how valuable that time had been, and I made an effort to be in whatever play or musical was happening each year after that. I even met my wife in college while doing a musical. God continued to strategically place people in my life to plant spiritual seeds in, as well as people to make an impact on the direction of my life.

Being in a play gives you the unique opportunity to spend hours together with the other actors everyday. You see them on their good days and their bad days. You experience success and failure together. You learn what motivates them and the things that they care about. It's a two way street though; they get to know you in all of these ways too. The more that they see you in different circumstances, the more they begin to see Jesus' light shining through you. As Christians, we are called to be salt and light to the earth, and what better way to influence your peers than to build relationships and friendships that can serve as grounds to share about Jesus?

Get Involved

The best way to reach out to theatre students is to get involved in a play yourself. You may have already been thinking about trying out for a play anyway, so now you have no excuse! You will be amazed at the amount of opportunities that God gives you to connect with other people through theatre. You spend many evenings with the other actors during months of rehearsals, and you'll find that there is a lot of conversation that goes on backstage in the green room.

If you're worried about acting or saying lines, but still want to get involved so that you can have those opportunities to talk to others about Jesus, consider helping out in a different way. Every play needs stage managers, set designers, and other similar roles. Pick up a paintbrush and volunteer to help create the scenery!

Show Your Support

It's not very fun to perform to an empty room. Theatre students thrive on sharing what they have been working on with others. Go see a play! Even better, invite your friends, family, and youth group to come show support. One of the best gifts you can give anybody is the gift of time. By giving your time, you are showing theatre students you genuinely care about them, and appreciate what interests them.

If you want to make somebody's day and really show them you care, look for people in the play that have supporting roles and not very many lines. Pay attention to what they did well in the performance. After a play, the theatre cast usually will stand in the hallway to greet the audience as they leave. Usually, the main characters get the most attention, but you will rock somebody's world if you make the effort to give specific and genuine compliments to people that had a supporting role and few lines. You may be the only person that talked to them, and that's not something that they will easily forget.

Having a Conversation

Here are a couple conversation topics to get you started:

- **What got you into theatre?** Through sharing the experiences that got them into theatre, they might share insight into their background. You can use what you learn to ask about other parts of their past.

- **What do you like most about theatre?** When you ask somebody about something that they enjoy and are passionate about, it will give you connection points to extend the conversation. They might even ask you what you like to do, at which point you can share about enjoying being part of the Church. Invite them to come with you sometime.

- **What is your favorite play and why?** Their favorite play can reveal what it is that they value. This could lead into a discussion about your favorite stories, at which point you can bring up your testimony and God's story.

- **If you could be one character from any play or movie, who would it be? Why?** A lot can be learned about a person when you learn who their role models are. They might ask you who you would be, and you could share with them about how you are trying to be more like Jesus.

- **If there was a play written about you, and you were the main character, how would you describe yourself? What parts about him or her do you like and what would you change?** We all want to be the hero, but many times we feel like the supporting role or even the villain. Their answer can reveal insight into their perception of themselves. This can be a great way to share encouragement, and the good news that Jesus is the solution.

42

- **I like to think of our lives as one big story. What's your story?** This is one of the best questions that you can ask somebody. They might not be willing to share much about themselves unless you have built a relationship with them, but if they do, you will learn a lot about the influences and choices that have made them who they are today. Pay attention, and don't be so anxious to tell your story that you ignore what they are saying. If you are genuinely interested in what they are saying, you will begin to see them through God's eyes and love them with God's heart.

- **What if all of history was one big dramatic play? Who would the writer be? What is the plot? How will the story end? How big are our rolls?** You may get some creative answers here, and that's good. In a sense, all of history is one big drama—God's drama. Have some fun with your friends, and be ready to share one possible view—that God is the playwright, and redemption through Christ is the plot. The story ends in different ways depending on the choice of the characters. And even though there are many roles, we are all in the center of God's stage.

GOD
SO
LOVED....

<u>5</u>

VOCALISTS

Lee Rogers

"Hey Ryan! Check this out!" I called enthusiastically.

Ryan came around the corner, "Whoa! We discovered the jackpot! This is just what we need."

"I know," I replied. "This will keep things interesting."

Travis walked in. "Yes! Awesome!" He exclaimed.

Each of us picked up a small clear plastic baggie and hurriedly began filling it with the candies of our choice. We were exploring the campus during a 20-minute break from choir practice, and discovered this bakery with an awesome candy selection. We had traveled to this small college as a select delegation of vocalists from our high school to participate in Honors Choir. Each year, choir directors from many of the area high schools brought a few of their best singers to participate.

We enjoyed this trip every year; it was fun to be together and to get out of school for two days. The singing was good too, but Honors Choir also meant two days of eight-hour rehearsals, learning complicated and challenging songs by renowned composers. For a student like me, with an extremely short attention span, any diversion was a welcomed one, so we bought candy. When our bags were full, we weighed in and paid the cashier, quickly hustling back to the concert hall to continue rehearsal. We shoved the bags of candy into our pockets, grabbed our music folders, and returned to our rows on the stage. Soon we were singing again.

The three of us had different vocal parts, so we didn't get to stand together on the stage. But we could still see each other, and each of us couldn't help but snicker as we began to slip candy discreetly into our mouths as rehearsal continued. It didn't take long for the students next to us to begin asking for candy, and we began to share. Soon 12 to 15 students in three distinct pockets of the choir occasionally raised a hand to their mouth, slipped in a gummy worm or a Sour Patch Kid or a Swedish Fish, and chewed while attempting to sing.

It didn't take long before one of the high school choir directors, seated in the hall observing the rehearsal, noticed something peculiar going on. She had been enjoying the music, but I saw the look on her face as it began to change from contentment to curiosity, and then from curiosity to a scowl. I knew we were caught, which made me laugh even more, almost to the point of losing control. Soon she had risen from her seat and was pointing an accusing finger in Ryan's direction. Some of us could not contain it any longer, and our stifled laughter began to spill out. Unwilling to interrupt the respected conductor, who was so focused on the music that he did not see what was going on, the grumpy choir teacher stormed out of the back of the concert hall, and we all breathed a sigh of relief as we continued to munch on candy while going through rehearsal.

At the end of the two days of rehearsal, we held the concert, and our voices joined together to create beautiful and powerful harmonies. At the end of the night, we returned home, most of us falling asleep during the van ride. Honors Choir was over until next year, but the memories we made would last a lifetime.

It seems like singing is more popular today than ever before. American Idol, The Voice, The X Factor, and The Sing-Off are all popular reality television shows dedicated to discovering and showcasing the singing talents and abilities of everyday people. Networks create these shows because they know they will draw in a large audience. American idol was the most watched show on television for six years in a row![1] Americans love good singing, whether they have the talent or not.

Because of the popularity of the art, it makes perfect sense to share Jesus with vocalists. You'll often find them in choir, in a musical, or at voice lessons. If you are a vocalist, develop friendships with your fellow singers by having fun together. Singing brought Ryan, Travis, and I together, but our friendship came from spending time together. Those friendships are the perfect platform for sharing Jesus. If you're not a vocalist, you can still serve and share Jesus with the vocalists in your school.

God loves singing! Psalm 96:1-2 declares, "Oh sing to the Lord a new song; sing to the Lord, all the earth! Sing to the Lord, bless his name; tell of his salvation from day to day."[2] God loves to be worshiped through singing, and when we glorify God through our voices by singing His praises, we "tell of his salvation." Not only that, but Scripture also demonstrates that God can respond to our singing with power that can change the circumstances around us, and transform us from the inside out. In Acts 16, Paul and Silas found themselves in prison for the sake of the Gospel. Shackled in chains, they began to sing praises to God around midnight. In response to their singing, God shook the jail with an earthquake, and the prison doors swung open as the chains fell from Paul and Silas' wrists. As a result of all that happened, the jailer and his entire family found salvation by believing in Jesus Christ. I'm not saying that your singing will cause an earthquake, but God could use your talent to start a God conversation with a fellow singer, and that conversation could shake their life and lead to their salvation.

Take Notice and Celebrate

Singing is an art, and like any art, a certain amount of natural ability will get you started, but vocal skills are honed through practice, study, and discipline. Unlike athletics, which are usually practiced in a group and in public, vocalists often train alone and behind closed doors, so their hard work usually goes unnoticed until the day of the performance. You can serve the vocalists in your life by taking notice of their talent and hard work, and then celebrate it! Attend their concerts and congratulate them on a good job. Take them out for pizza afterward to celebrate, or give them a shout out on social media. If you have a Bible Club in your school, consider reaching out to the vocalists by throwing them an 'after party' following their major concerts. You can have games, food, and a karaoke machine—they will love it!

Serve Together Through Singing

One of my favorite memories with my fellow vocalists in high school was going Christmas caroling. Ryan was two years ahead of me in school, and when he called to invite me I was really excited. It was awesome that an upperclassman took notice and thought enough of me to invite me along. If you are a vocalist, invite your fellow singers to carol with you. If you're a senior or junior, take a special interest in the lowerclassmen, because you can have a great amount of influence in their lives.

You can also invite them to visit a local nursing home with you, and sing to the elderly there throughout the year, not just at Christmas. It may seem like an odd thing to do, but most people will find serving others a rewarding experience once they've done it. Caroling or visiting a nursing home together not only serves the people you are singing to, but it also creates the perfect opportunity to share your motivation for serving—Jesus Christ.

Invite Them Into the Body of Christ

You should invite your vocalist friends to join you in singing at church in the choir, or in your youth group. Some vocalists will already have a church they sing with, but many will not. Inviting them into participation with the Body of Christ through singing might just be the connection they need to place their faith in Jesus. Today people need to belong before they can believe, so help them believe in Jesus by inviting them to belong to your church choir or youth group worship team. If you are involved in any kind of Fine Arts Festival through your church or youth group, invite your vocalist friends to participate! You'll be sharing Jesus with them through their participation in the Body of Christ, and they will also be enriching the church by adding their gifts and abilities to it.

Listen to the Lyrics—Then Start a Discussion

One of my favorite songs from Honors Choir was Psalm 23 by Carl Nygard, a local composer. Mr. Nygard even directed the choir personally when we sang this Psalm. When we sang together in the school chorus, we weren't just singing any old songs. We frequently sang songs about God, because most of the classical and renowned musical pieces in Western civilization were created by, and for, the church. In order to give students the fullest musical education, schools must engage these songs with their bands and choirs. If you are in choir, and you are singing a song about God, take the time to have a conversation with your friends about the lyrics. Throughout the conversation, listen to their perspective of the lyrics, and be ready to share your own.

Having a Conversation

Like many activities you may be involved in at school, choir creates an environment for good friendships and great conversations. Here are some questions to get you started on a powerful conversation with a vocalist that can lead to Jesus:

- **How did you get started in singing? Tell me about it.** This is a great 'get to know you' question. It can help you develop a friendship by learning about your fellow singer's past involvement with music. You will have the opportunity to share how you got started in singing too, and if you started with singing in the church, be sure to bring it up.

- **What does singing mean to you? What does being involved in the choir mean to you?** Jump into their interest in singing by asking these questions. Oftentimes, vocalists find their identity in their voice, and in having their voices heard. You can bring value to them by discussing this identity, and what they get out of it. Be ready to share what singing means to you, especially how you worship God and what significance that has in your life.

- **What do you think about coming with me to sing in church sometime? Would you join my church choir with me?** Invite your friend to use their talent in full participation in the Body of Christ. Get them into a church atmosphere. After they've been involved for a few weeks, have a discussion about what church means to you, and what it means to them.

- **What did you think about those lyrics?** When you sing a song about God in your choir or chorus, ask your fellow vocalist friend about the significance of the lyrics. Have a discussion about God by talking together about the meaning behind the words. Discuss what the words mean to you, and what they could mean for your friend. Use this discussion to share the Gospel.

---

[1] https://en.m.wikipedia.org/wiki/Nielsen_ratings#Top-rated_programs.
[2] ESV.

GOD SO LOVED....

<u>6</u>
BASKETBALL PLAYERS
Ben Russell

I will never forget what it felt like to walk back into that gymnasium—the one I had played basketball in for four years. Ten years later the logo in the middle of the court was faded, but the gym smelled exactly the same. I was back, but this time as an assistant coach. A dream of mine was coming true—I was back at my alma mater coaching the sport I loved so much!

At the first practice, there was a young man (we will call him James) who was a senior and a shooting guard. It became very obvious to me that James was by far the best player on the court. Before the official practice began, the team was shooting shots and getting loose. I was standing near James as he was shooting; he pulled up from the 3 point line for a shot—swish! He looked at me and smiled, and then he winked. I quickly realized that he had a swagger about him, a confidence; this kid was on a different level from anyone else.

James was a great basketball player, and he knew it. That combination has the potential to be bad for any basketball team. That first practice was interesting; James was intense the entire time—yelling at his teammates, taking shots when he was covered (ball-hogging is what it's called in basketball terms), and generally ignoring everything that myself or the other coach would tell him.

The most ironic thing about James was how respectful he was off the court to everyone. But when he played basketball, he was completely different. The first couple weeks of practice were just like the first. James trash-talked his fellow players when he scored on them, and yelled when they did something wrong. It was really beginning to bother the rest of the team. It was also affecting their morale. The head coach, my good and longtime friend, pulled me aside. "I need you to make James your project this season. He needs some type of guidance. Can you use your experience with students to help mentor him?"

"I will give it a try," I said. So I started having more conversations with James before and after practice. I asked him about school, life, and anything else I could think of, and he really opened up to me. He talked about his girlfriend and where he would take her on dates, and of course we talked a lot about basketball. We developed a pretty good friendship in a short period of time. Things were progressing, and I was glad. I liked James, and I felt I was making a difference in him. It seemed that way by his attitude, at least.

The first game of the season was an away game, and we were playing a team far less talented than ours. At half time, we had a good lead, and James, of course, had played fantastic. I remember he had somewhere around 15 points with a few assists. We were huddled in the locker room when, out of nowhere, James' dad burst in yelling at him—claiming he should have scored more points, played better defense, and that he wasn't running fast enough down the court. Our head coach kindly asked the dad to leave the locker room. I glanced over at James. Tears were swelling in his eyes and his head dropped; he was humiliated. The MVP of our team had just been scolded in public by the person who should have been his biggest supporter; his father.

It became very obvious that James acted the way he did on the court because he had so much pressure from his dad. His swagger and confidence weren't only because he played the game so well; they were also a cover up. Many basketball players display an attitude of over-confidence and sometimes arrogance, but it is often a screen to cover insecurity, fear, or challenges that are not obvious to everyone. Not every student who plays basketball has the kind of problems James had, but they all have needs and could benefit from someone speaking encouragement into their lives. God is calling you to stand in the gap for people just like James and others on your basketball team. The MVP, the player who barely made the team, and all the rest deserve to have someone give them encouragement, just like I did with James.

Think about the people who stood in the gap for others in the Bible; they all had a specific calling about the situation they were in. Here are just a few examples:[1]

- Nehemiah identified a problem to solve in Nehemiah 2.
- Noah was "all in," no matter the cost in Genesis 5.
- John the Baptist was willing to take risks in Matthew 3.

God is calling you to each of these as well. Let's take a closer look.

Identify The Problem

Jerusalem fell to the Babylonians, and 141 years later (yes, you read that correctly, 141 years later) God's people were still in distress. The walls of their city had been destroyed and still laid in ruins. Nehemiah knew this was a problem, and he was ready to do something about it. He answered God's call. After much time in prayer, he asked the king if he could rebuild those walls, and the king said yes!

I've often wondered why it took 141 years for someone not only to see the need, but also to be willing to do something about it. What is the need on your basketball team? I would encourage you to write down three things that seem to be the biggest needs on your team. Don't wait around for someone else to identify the problems—be proactive. If you don't identify the problem, maybe no one will!

Be "All In"

If you have grown up in church, you are probably familiar with the story of Noah. It was one of the first Bible stories I ever remember hearing as a child. In case you aren't familiar, the following is the story in short. God planned to flood the earth because of the wickedness of man, but chose to save Noah by having him build a huge boat. It took Noah 120 years to do so, and his neighbors mocked him during the process. When the floods came, he loaded up his family with some animals and was safe. Everything else was destroyed, but Noah heard from God and was obedient.

Noah demonstrated incredible faith even though everyone else was filled with fear. For this to take place there could be no middle ground. Noah either obeyed God, or he didn't! He spent those 120 years begging people to turn back to God. He was all in! Genesis 6:9 defines him perfectly, "Noah was a righteous man, blameless among the people of his time, and he walked faithfully with God."[2] There was no turning back for Noah. He lived in very hard times, when people were far from God, but he remained obedient!

It's one thing to be obedient to God for a short time; it's entirely something else to be faithful for the long haul. Be all in for reaching your basketball team. The surroundings may be tough, but Noah made it, you can too! Being all in means being consistent, as well. Try to set up a meeting with the team's head coach to see how you can serve your basketball team on a regular basis. Often stat keepers, water boys/girls, ball boys/girls are volunteer students. You never know what the avenue could be for you to go "all in."

Take a Risk

I felt building a friendship with James was a risk. He might of thought I was weird, and could have pushed me further away. I still felt it was worth a shot, and I am glad I did. John the Baptist is a great example of being a risk-taker. John's job was to get people ready for Jesus and lead them to repentance. By the way, John was also known to smell bad, wear weird clothes, and eat very strange food. Still, he was a popular public speaker, telling people to turn from their wicked ways. Seems pretty risky to me!

I'm certainly not telling you to start smelling bad, or to eat odd food, but the example we have of John's bravery should be very motivating. Some people will join us following God with all our hearts, but others will think we've lost our minds. It's worth the risk to talk to them about it. You don't have to be the most athletic person around to share Jesus with the basketball team. But you do have to be willing to take a risk! I encourage you to start a conversation with a team member that leads to Jesus. Get past the awkwardness and take that risk – it could be a very rewarding conversation.

Having a Conversation

Basketball has been part of my life for as long as I can remember. My 5-year-old son plays basketball right now. There's a soft spot in my heart for those who play the game. I've coached dozens of young men who needed a relationship with Jesus in their lives. I want to encourage you to stand in the gap for the basketball teams at your school. Just like I did with James, start a conversation with them. Here are a few questions that could lead to a powerful conversation:

- **What got you started playing basketball?** This is a great way to find out about your friend's past. Understanding his past may help you better understand where he is today. This basketball opener can lead to more questions about the past.

- **What's the most rewarding part about playing basketball? What makes it so rewarding?** Listen and learn from the responses you hear. If can make a connection, talk about the rewarding experience of following Christ and being a part of the Church. Invite them to join you sometime.

- **Outside of a basketball coach, who has had the most influence on your life?** This actually may make them stutter a bit. A lot of basketball players would say a coach here, so taking that out will tell you about other influences in their lives. When it's your turn, be sure to talk about Jesus and the Church and the influence they have on your life.

---

[1] De Jesus, Wilfredo, *In The Gap* (Springfield, MO: Influence Resources, 2014) 19.
[2] NIV.

GOD

SO

LOVED....

7

CHEERLEADERS

Jessica Riner

I was a cheerleader in high school. We had several girls on our cheer team for basketball and football season. It was way more stressful being on the team than I ever thought it would be. When I used to watch the cheerleaders from the stands it looked fun, energetic, and all the cheers seemed to be in rhythm. I did not realize at the time how much hard work the girls put in during practice times to be able to look great when they were cheering our team on. Our coach was rough in the way she talked to us, always yelling at us to, "Get those arms up! Keep those arms tight and straight!" I wondered if I would ever be able to please our coach. Some girls seemed to have just the right moves, while I struggled daily to get it right. There is so much pressure on cheerleaders to be perfectly in sync with the rest of the team.

Cheerleaders put in many hours of hard work each week. However, they are often overlooked and unappreciated for the work they do. They bring so much energy and excitement to the game as they cheer the team on. They work hard at encouraging the people in the stands to be excited with them. When you show even a little appreciation for their efforts this will go a long way in connecting with the heart of every cheerleader.

Dear brothers and sisters, when troubles of any kind come your way, consider it an opportunity for great joy. For you know that when your faith is tested, your endurance has a chance to grow. So let it grow, for when your endurance is fully developed, you will be perfect and complete, needing nothing.
James 1:2-4 NLT

Therefore, since we are surrounded by such a huge crowd of witnesses to the life of faith, let us strip off every weight that slows us down, especially the sin that so easily trips us up. And let us run with endurance the race God has set before us.
Hebrews 12:1 NLT

In these verses we are encouraged to allow endurance to develop within us. To be a great cheerleader, a person has to develop the skill of endurance. The Cambridge Dictionary describes endurance as the ability to keep doing something difficult, unpleasant, or painful for a long time.[1] Cheerleaders must be able to withstand days of long practices so they can be their best on the field or on the court.

In my own journey as a cheerleader, over time I was able to build up muscles and strength which helped me become a better cheerleader. It took a lot of hard work, but it was worth the effort. You can be an encouragement to any cheerleader by acknowledging their level of endurance in their sport. Let them know how much you appreciate their willingness to press through the difficult days.

I mentioned to you earlier how difficult in was to serve under our head cheerleading coach, but it was much different with our assistant coach. Coach D—as we called her—was fun, loving, and an encouragement to us all. She truly seemed to care about every girl on the team. All the girls loved hanging out with her. She was also one of the youth leaders at a local church in my town.

One Wednesday evening I went with a friend to Coach D's youth ministry. That night changed my life forever. I think Coach D knew I had been struggling on the team. I believe she also knew that I needed something greater than talent to survive the school year. Towards the end of the service, she sat down beside me and begin to ask me a series of questions. One question led to another.

"Do you have any friends that we could pray for tonight? Do you have any friends who need Jesus in their life?" Coach D asked. I began to share names of students that I knew who were struggling through family issues or school drama. Then very gently she directed the questions towards me. "Jessica, what about you? Have you ever accepted Jesus into your life? Would you like to give your heart to Jesus, tonight?"

That conversation with Coach D forever shaped my life because I chose in that moment to say yes to Jesus. The peace and joy that filled my heart, as I surrendered my life to Jesus, is what every student is longing to experience.

Do Not Be Intimidated

I know sometimes cheerleaders get a bad reputation or may seem hard to connect with in a conversation. However, I want to encourage you—a student who loves Jesus—to have a conversation with a cheerleader in your school. Cheerleaders are students in your school, just like every other student. While they may be in the popular crowd because of the lime-light they walk in, they are still students who are in need of a relationship with Jesus. Do not allow fear to keep you from having an incredible conversation with one of the cheerleaders in your school.

No one at my school had ever asked me about having a relationship with Jesus. Many of them assumed that because I went to church, I was already a Christian. I am so thankful Coach D asked me if I wanted to give my life to Jesus. I want to encourage you to share Jesus with your friends at school. Do not allow their talents or sports abilities to intimidate you. You have the answers they are searching for in this life. Having a conversation with you about how Jesus has made a difference in your life may be the very thing that causes your friend to open up and accept Jesus Christ as their Lord and Savior

Show That You Care

Let the love of Christ shine through you to the cheerleaders in your school. If you want to begin a conversation that leads to Jesus with a cheerleader in your school, first show them that you care. Caring for others opens the door for you to share Christ with them. Here are some ways you can serve the cheerleaders in your school and show them that you care:

- Get together with a few of your friends and make goodie bags for the cheerleaders. Snicker bars or a protein bar and sports drinks or bottles of water along with a hand-written thank you note will go a long way in showing appreciation.
- Take a cooler of ice filled with water and sports drinks to a home game for the team to enjoy. Attach a note of thanks for all they do for the school team.
- Put posters up in their bus for the away games that say things like:
  o Our school appreciates you.
  o You are valuable.
  o Thank you for all you do to encourage the team.
  o Go _____! (name the school team name)

Having a Conversation

Get to know the cheerleader by learning to ask good questions:

- Ask about their practice times. How did practice go this week with your team? Did you learn any new cheers? What cheer is your favorite?
- Ask about the games. What do you enjoy most about cheering at games? What is the most frustrating thing about cheering during a game? Let them know you will be praying for them during the next game and remember to actually pray.
- Ask what they like to do for fun. Plan a day for them to hang out with you and some friends.
- Ask if they have any brothers or sisters. Find out about their family life.
- Who is one person that has been influential in your life?
- Can I share a story with you of a person who has greatly influenced my life forever? Be ready to share how Jesus has influenced your life.
- Share your favorite scripture verse with them and tell them why it is your favorite.

- Ask them if they would like to know Jesus in a personal way. You may just lead the next youth pastor or missionary to the Lord.
- Invite them to attend your local youth ministry with you.

---

[1] "Endurance." Cambridge Dictionary.
https://dictionary.cambridge.org/us/dictionary/english/endurance

GOD
SO
LOVED....

8
FOOTBALL PLAYERS

Forrest Rowell

I was born and raised in Pueblo, Colorado, a community of about 110,000 located at the southern end of the Front Range of the Rocky Mountains. We're fairly close to where the prairie ends and the mountains begin. Pueblo has plenty of history, more than can be shared here and now, but one interesting fact about Pueblo has to do with football. We have the oldest high school football rivalry west of the Mississippi, and it centers on the Centennial Bulldogs and the Central Wildcats. Every year they face off in the "Bell Game"—a game I dreamed about playing in since I was a kid.

I grew up in a house full of sisters, and while I hung out with them occasionally, most of the time I got on their last nerves. I remember one time they had some friends over at the house. They were in their room talking about whatever girls talk about, while I was outside the door making noise and being obnoxious. That seems to be the younger brother's job—to be a professional nuisance to his older sisters. Finally, Sunshine, my older sister, opened the door. She quickly moved past me, around the corner, and up the stairs. "Keep that little jerk away from us!" I heard her scream to our mother at the top of her lungs.

I was right behind her when I interjected, "No, mom. I'm not a little jerk; I'm a *big* jerk!" Thinking I was the pinnacle of comedy, I began to laugh hysterically. Surprisingly, my mom and sister joined in, but after the laughter subsided they were back to business.

"Keep him away from us," Sunshine said to my mother in all seriousness.

I really was a little dude, slightly under-sized, and I always had a desire to be "BIG." Some jokingly refer to that condition as the "Napoleon Complex." As I grew older, I found that athletics came fairly natural to me, so I played as many sports as I could. football, baseball, soccer, tennis, hockey, wrestling, and track—just to name a few. I'll never forget one afternoon when I was picked up from football practice, shoulder pads and pants still on, only to jump out of the car a few minutes later with my bag of hockey gear in hand.

Now that you have just a little insight of my background, let's get back to the topic at hand—FOOTBALL! I love and respect most every sport, but there's something special about football. I'm not sure what it is or how to describe it, but it's incredibly significant to me. Now I know that football players tend to be labeled with several stereotypes: wild partiers, gym rats, meatheads, cocky, or dumb jocks. These are some of the common misconceptions. Yes, there are usually one or two bad apples, but they tend to spoil the bunch. The truth is, many football players are highly focused individuals; we are driven by our love and desire to play the game and we will do whatever is necessary to be able to play.

Many athletes do what they do because of a God-given passion to compete in whatever arena they are called to. We are competitive warriors that train endless hours to prove ourselves on the field. A focused football player endures great amounts of pain—blood, sweat, and tears—to play the game. We are coached that there is no substitute for aggressive effort for success! It's not all about the work, but it is about the work ethic! A well coached football player understands how to be stoked, but not satisfied—always wanting to become just a little bigger, faster, and stronger. Anybody can watch football, but only few have the guts to play football.

Nowadays, I serve as a Youth Alive Missionary in the Rocky Mountains and I have been given some amazing opportunities to stand before athletes ranging from 5-18 years old. Every time I'm in a setting like that I've found it helpful to communicate a message that inspires them in the areas of *challenge, winning and losing, or team.*

Challenge

Colossians 3:23 reads, "Work willingly at whatever you do, as though you were working for the Lord rather than for people." (NLT) When communicating to a football player, and many other athletes, it's important to challenge them to play above themselves. Not simply for their own glory, not for the glory of the team, or the coaches, but for the glory of God! Athletes don't mind a challenge—as a matter fact they tend to thrive on challenges.

Here's one simple idea about how your youth ministry or your campus club can challenge the football team at your school. Most football players love, and I mean LOVE to eat! Ask the Coach early in the season, or even before the season starts, if you could purchase, prepare, serve, and clean up a meal for his players. Offer to pray for the football team at that meal—for a victory and for safety—and challenge them with God's word. Challenge them to not only play the game of football at a higher level, but also the game of life.

Winning and Losing

Philippians 4:13 states, "For I can do everything through Christ, who gives me strength."[1] Another characteristic of football players, and many other athletes, is they know about winning and losing. They know how great it feels to win, and how devastating it feels to lose. Winning is obviously better then losing, so challenge football players to not only win on the field, but also how to win in eternity.

You can serve the football team when they win or lose with your Bible Club, or just as a group of Campus Missionaries. When they win, encourage them by creating a banner that congratulates the team for a job well done. The banner could be displayed in a school hallway where they will see it and appreciate the acknowledgment. Include a favorite Bible verse that talks about being victorious. If they lose, still encourage them with a banner that shows your support. Let them know that you are with them whether they win or lose.

Team

Ecclesiastes 4:12 reads, "A person standing alone can be attacked and defeated, but two can stand back-to-back and conquer. Three are even better, for a triple-braided cord is not easily broken."[2] Athletes understand team; let them know how to join the winning team. Jesus and his disciples were a great team! Jesus provided salvation for all mankind, and the disciples spread that message across the known world. That team continues today as the Church. Invite your football-playing friends to church with you. Invite them to join your youth group team. Invite them to join Jesus' team!

Having a Conversation

Three great topics to start a conversation with a football player are the same topics mentioned above: challenge, winning and losing, and team. Here are a few questions for great conversations:

- **What's the biggest game you've ever played in? What did it feel like?** This is a simple question to get to know a football player better. Listen to their story, when they get pumped, or mention something interesting, ask them about it.

- **What's the most challenging part of the game of football? What makes it so challenging? What do you learn from it?** Listen to their response, and admire what they have to share with you. You can even transition this conversation into life by asking, "What's the most challenging part of life?"

- **When you play football, what are you playing for? Have you ever been challenged to play for someone or something bigger then yourself?** Find out their heart and motivation with the first question, and then share your heart with the second question. Share that you're striving to do all things for Christ, and that you find it to be the greatest challenge of them all. Invite your friend to join you in the challenge.

- **How important is team and teamwork to a football player? What does a good team with good teamwork do for one another?** A football team won't win much without good teamwork. They need each other if they are going to do well. Life in Christ is also about teamwork, as we are a part of the church. In fact, the Apostle Paul says the church is like a physical body, and all the members are different parts of the body. The body can't function without it's parts. Use this question to connect to a discussion about the church, your role, and how you'd love to see your friend join in.

- **What have you had to sacrifice for your teammates? What role does sacrifice play in victory?** As a Christian, I'm sure you recognize the word sacrifice. This is a word familiar to football players, also. Listen to their perspective on this, and then share some perspective of your own. The following illustration can help guide you. The sacrifice an offensive player makes on the field, particularly the lineman, is so the quarterback or running back can make a great play. In the same way, Jesus sacrificed himself for us so that we could also win a victory over sin, hell, and the grave.

---

[1] NLT.
[2] NLT.

GOD
SO
LOVED....

9
SOCCER PLAYERS

Anthony Lecocq

My first thought was "Whose blood is this?" It was the last game of my high school soccer career, and I had just had a midair head-on head collision vying for a header with a defender from the opposing team (I still have a half-circle scar from his upper row of teeth). We were wearing our home kits, which I loved, because they were all white and were as savage as jerseys could be back in 2006. But when I came to, my jersey was stained bright red, and my hair was soaking wet with blood. I was helped up and taken to the ambulance on the side of the field. Full of adrenaline, I asked the paramedics over and over if I could go back in the game, until they finally said, "You probably need stitches, but go ahead." I played the last 5 minutes. We lost 4-3. It's funny to me now, but at the time I sat in the locker room and cried, because the game meant so much to me. When I left the locker room, I drove myself to the emergency room and got five staples in my head.

The soccer pitch has been a place of spiritual highs and lows for me. It's been a place where I've influenced people and people have influenced me; a place where I shared my faith with teammates and a place where obscene things have come out of my mouth. I've led my team in prayer on the soccer pitch, and I once punched a stranger in a bench-clearing brawl. Sometimes your mission field and your wilderness of temptation are the same place.

I went through a spiritual transition during my freshman year. God was convicting and stirring and tug-of-warring me out of being a lukewarm Christian, and into a bolder faith. I wasn't really the most popular guy to begin with, so as I stopped going with the flow of my friends' sin, my friendships got thinner and thinner. I had to stop hanging out with a couple guys completely on weekends because they were getting really into drinking and messing around with girls. One day, while lined up during a shooting drill, those guys took turns spitting on my back over and over until I noticed. I was obviously upset. The Lord helped me react calmly, but I was very hurt and felt so alone on my team.

I didn't understand then that my friends were frustrated at my lifestyle. They didn't understand me, but they were curious. People don't always know what to do with you when you're different. But you have to be different to make a difference! Talents aside, you are the Most Valuable Player on your team. Being different makes you valuable.

In Matthew 5:13-16, Jesus began His biggest recorded teaching, The Sermon on The Mount, by giving identity to his followers. He chose a metaphor that some people don't understand. "You are the Salt of the Earth. But what good is salt if it has lost its flavor? Can you make it salty again? It will be thrown out and trampled underfoot as worthless."[1]

Salt creates thirst in people, adds flavor to bland things, and preserves things from decay. In Jesus' time, before refrigerators and electrical outlets, rubbing salt into meat was the primary way to keep it from spoiling. Jesus mentions that some salt "loses its flavor." The word he uses is the Greek word "*moranthay*," which also means "has grown foolish" or "has become infatuated."

What's this mean for my identity on my team? Well, your faith in Christ adds the flavor of life to an otherwise bland sinful existence. Jesus is the salt in you, and overflowing with Him will certainly create thirst for God on your soccer team.

When we have stopped being different, we have lost our usefulness in the Kingdom of God, and are like that salt that is trampled underfoot as worthless. Guard your heart from going with the foolish flow of the world, and don't become infatuated with the lifestyles of your teammates.

The Gospel has an interesting way of bringing out the fighter in us. Before you know it you're desperate to participate in it for one more minute (even if your head is bleeding). My prayer for you is that you wouldn't just feed them brilliant 'through' balls and crosses, but the salt of a life lived for Jesus; that their hearts would burn within them for something more, and that you would make the most of every opportunity.

Be a Simple Blessing

Blessing a soccer team is a huge open door. In an American context, soccer typically takes a backseat to other sports, so giving a little attention to a program goes a long way. Players are very thirst conscious. "Hydrate or die-drate," as they say. One way of being a simple blessing is to provide a couple packs of cold Gatorades for the team. Ask the coach if he or she will allow you to share an encouragement, pray for the team, or promote an upcoming Bible Club event or outreach.

Be a Fanbase

Most of my classmates never came to one soccer game. We would come out of the locker room and into our massive football stadium to find only 30 parents in the crowd. We would jokingly say, "Another sold out crowd." If you want to impact a squad, all you have to do is show up! Make a sign, bring a broom to cheer on the sweeper, buy some vuvuzelas. Bring the entire Bible Club with you, or your youth group. Don't be ignorant or obnoxious, but let your voice be heard!

Be a Big Blessing

Soccer players burn a lot of energy on the field, and they need a lot of fuel to last an entire game at their best. That fuel comes from good food, and you can be a big blessing by providing it for them. If you offer to provide an after school team meal before a game, the coaches won't even know how to respond. They will be floored! They might even think you're trying to trick them, but you can ensure your sincerity by asking what kinds of foods would be best for the team. Ask the coaches if you can pray for the team at the meal and share an encouraging Scripture with them. If it goes well, be an even bigger blessing by making the meal a regular thing.

It's the Little Things

Most schools can't afford to buy their players matching cleats. Your Bible Club probably can't afford it, either. But you could take a smaller step by getting the team matching shoelaces! What are your school colors? Find some laces online that would match them and buy enough for the entire team. Drop them off to the coach at practice one day with a note from your Bible Club.

Be a Mini Blessing

You've probably seen the miniature soccer balls that fit in your hand, but you probably don't know that dribbling skills get developed when you use a smaller ball. I'm not talking about the small foam balls the size of a hacky sack, but actual inflatable mini soccer balls about the size of a grapefruit. Soccer players know—if they can do it with a grapefruit, it'll be simple with a full sized ball. You could buy every player a small ball and sharpie 2 scripture verses on each one.

Having a Conversation

Leaders Hold The Keys: Questions To Ask Your Coach

- **Can I be our team's chaplain?** You're asking to share a Scripture and pray with the team before games, or after practices.

- If you skip a practice or have to leave early for a worship event, make sure you communicate to your coaches in advance and ask, **"Can I come early to get my sprints out of the way?"**

- If you are penalized with a lack of a starting position or playing time, don't argue with your coaches, but ask, **"How can I work harder to improve to a starting position?"**

Be Invitational: No One Can Say Yes If You Don't Invite Them!

- **Do you want a ride to/from practice? Do you want to get food after?** Connect with your teammates and develop a deeper relationship off the field.

- **I'm planning a Saturday team breakfast, can you come?** Serve your entire team—and invite each player personally.

- **Do you have a free period, before or after school for a team-lifting session?** Build your team's unity by getting them together for extra workouts.

- **Will you go with me to FCA, or another school-based Christian Club event, or my student ministry?** Invite them into fellowship with the Body of Christ on the school campus.

When You Have Real Talk:

- **What are your off-the-field goals for this year?** Be ready to share yours to—including your goals for spiritual growth.

- **Who are you giving 'assists' to off the field?** Encourage your friend in helping others, and be ready to share about those you are helping, as well. Talk about your faith, and why assisting others is important to you.

- **If modern sports were all available, what sport do you think Jesus would have played?** This may seem like an odd question, but it's a great way to start talking about Jesus.

- **If you don't get to see out the dream of playing professional soccer, what do you want to do with your life?** Listen closely and sincerely to your friend. Get to know them better, and encourage them in their dreams. Be ready to share your own dream as well, and the role God plays in thinking about your future.

The most effective way to forge an influential friendship with a soccer teammate is to simply hang out with them. Take an interest in their life. Text them. Support them. Joke with them. Take the locker next to them in the locker room. Share your pre-wrap and shin guard tape. Listen to each other's pregame playlists. Go out of your way to get their ball when they shank one over the goal. Be the kind of person that's more interested in hearts than in trophies, and more interested in serving your team than racking up your own stats. And as you do, remember to talk about your faith and invite them into your life by inviting them to your Bible Club, youth group, or church.

---

[1] NLT.

GOD
SO
LOVED....

10

MY LUNCH TABLE

Jessica Riner

The one place a student has a captive audience at school is at the lunch table. Each day you have twenty to thirty minutes to talk to friends as you eat together. Many different conversations take place every day in the cafeteria. Navigating a conversation to bring Jesus to the center can be a little challenging at times, but it's always possible to find a way to share Jesus at school—especially over lunch.

It was a typical day at Jackson High School. Students were heading to the cafeteria to eat lunch. After paying for their meal, students began looking for a place to sit. Gracie and her friends all sat down together. Another classmate of Muslim background joined them at their table. They began having the usual conversations like most teens have over lunch; talking about what had happened on social media, their teachers, the latest school gossip, and plans for the weekend. Not long into their meal, Gracie's friends got up and headed to the vending machines, leaving her to finish her lunch. As her friends got up and left the table, the Holy Spirit nudged her and said, "Here is the divine appointment you have been praying for."

Earlier in the year Gracie had been praying for God to give her opportunities to witness to her friends, yet in this moment she was confused because all her friends had just got up and left. As she looked across the table the only person remaining was her Muslim classmate. Gracie responded by praying, "Ok God, I know, I know." She said she sensed God was about to do something in this classmate's life as they sat there eating lunch. The conversation, as told by Gracie, went a little like this:

Looking at other classmates and then back at Gracie, Hafi asked, "Why are you different from them?"

Gracie responded, "I am a Christian."

"I don't mean this in a bad way, but don't they claim to be Christians also? You are not involved in things they do. Why not?"

"Well, Christians are not supposed to do things like drink, smoke, etc., so I don't...if that answers your question," said Gracie.

"What are Christians supposed to do?" asked Hafi.

Gracie answered, "We are supposed to share the Gospel and love God's people."

"Wait, so...everyone? You love everyone? Even me? But I am a Muslim."

"Yes, Christians love Muslims. We are not supposed to judge or hate like many people make us out to do," said Gracie.

Still astonished, Hafi asked again, "So you love me, even though I am a Muslim?"

"Yes!" said Gracie. "God loves you too. He loves you more than you could ever think."

"But I thought Christians were taught to shame and hate those who are not Christian. That is what I have always heard," said Hafi.

Looking at her friend she said, "It is actually the opposite. We are supposed to love everyone. We are not to point at people and cast judgment because God loves everyone."

As Gracie continued to share her story with me, she said Hafi just smiled and changed the subject as the other students returned to the table. Little did she know, as she prayed for an opportunity, that God would widen her territory to plant seeds of His love while sitting at the lunch table.

The lunch table is a great place to strike up a conversation about Jesus with your friends. What conversation could the Lord be preparing for you to have with a friend this year over lunch? Will you be willing to let the Lord use you? Will you take a few moments during your school lunch to impact another life?

As I think about Gracie's story 1 John 4:19-20 comes to my mind. It says, *"We love because he first loved us. If anyone says, 'I love God,' yet hates his brother, he is a liar. For anyone who does not love his brother, whom he has seen, cannot love God, whom he has not seen."[1]* As a follower of Christ, we are to love everybody and show His love to them no matter who they are. We are all God's children. Everyone deserves the opportunity to hear about Christ. Only then can they make a decision to accept or reject his love. Your responsibility as a student is to let your friends know about Christ's love. Let God do the rest.

Sharing Jesus with your friends begins by earning the right to be heard by serving them. The following sections contain a few ideas for serving your table during lunch. You can do this by yourself or have a few friends join you in your efforts to reach your classmates. It is always great to bring others along for the journey and have them involved in serving your school. Remember to always pray over your efforts. Ask the Lord to bless whatever you are doing and to help you with conversations.

Buy Lunch

Buy a friend's lunch, sit with them, and begin a conversation to get to know them so you can eventually share Christ with them. This may take more than one try if it is a new person you are getting to know. The important thing to remember is this: you are beginning to make a new friend so that you have the right to speak into his or her life. A few Campus Missionaries did this at a school in Georgia one year and made an impact in their friends lives. It took buying lunch for their friends a few times before the students didn't mind listening and eventually began to attend the local youth group. The great thing is the campus missionaries did not give up after the first attempt to make a difference in a friend's life.

Bring Some Cookies

Everybody loves cookies! Hand out individually wrapped cookies one day during lunch with an invitation to your Bible club or to your local youth group service. Make sure to include the date, time, and location of the event. If you invited your friends to your Bible club, be ready to share a missional message that week—like your personal testimony. If you invited your friends to youth group, ask your youth pastor for a moment to share your testimony that week during the service. Or you can plan to take your friend out to eat after the youth service and share what Christ is doing in your life. Make sure to plan ahead.

Having a Conversation

Building a good foundation first is very important. You want to get to know the person and be able to navigate a great conversation. You don't want to come across as trying to cram Jesus down their throat in the short twenty minutes you have over lunch. The questions listed below are designed to help you break the ice and begin a conversation. These questions can build upon each other and eventually lead to talking about Jesus once you have gotten to know your new friend. However, if you are talking with a friend you have known for a while, the topic of Jesus may come up more quickly and more naturally in your conversation. The point is to be ready whenever your friend is open to discussing things about the Lord. Don't be frustrated if it takes time to lead into a conversation about Jesus. Your friends need to know that you care about them first and foremost. They will be more willing to listen to what you have to say as conversations progress in the future if you first take the time to get to know them. With that being said, here are a few questions to get you started towards a conversation that shares Jesus:

- **What has your day been like today?** The goal here is to find out what is going on in their life in the immediate.

- **What did you do this weekend? Did anything interesting happen?** This will tell you about their interests and activities. It may even give you knowledge of whether they attend church anywhere.

- **What are your plans after school today?** This will help you connect with them more and build a bridge of friendship, if you can hang out sometime beyond school.

- **What is one thing that is really important to you in life?** Find out what really matters to your friend. Maybe it is God, family, friends, sports, etc.

- **What makes _____ important to you?** Fill in the blank with whatever they just told you if they didn't already expand on their answer. What makes this subject important to your friend? Be a good listener. Also, be ready if they return the questions to you.

This could be a great moment to share about your faith in Christ and how important it is to you.

- **In your opinion, who is Jesus?** This is not to be an argumentative question. Just listen to what they believe about Jesus. Maybe they think he is the Son of God, a great teacher, someone they have never heard of, or the Savior of their life.

- **Can I share my story with you of how my life changed one day?** Be ready to share your story of how Jesus has impacted your life and the difference he has made in you.

---

[1] NIV.

GOD
SO
LOVED....

11

MINORITY STUDENTS

Peter and Joanna Reeves

Can you remember some of your favorite birthday parties you were invited to when you were young? There is nothing quite like the feeling of being handed an invitation to celebrate your friend's birthday! Being with your best friends at Chuck-E-Cheese, going bowling, or to the movies were some of our most fantastic childhood memories. My wife, Joanna, even had a farm come to her house for her birthday once, and all of her friends could pet the animals and ride ponies around her yard! Everyone loves to be invited to a party—and I'm no different.

I'll never forget the day that invitations were being passed around my 4th-grade classroom. It started out very exciting, but quickly changed from an exciting day to a day that left a scar on my heart for a really long time. It was a Friday in June and the thrill of the school year ending combined with Taylor's birthday coming up was a lot of excitement for a fourth grader! Tayler was a close friend of mine, and I had a crush on her. Taylor and I sat together at lunch, played with each other at recess, and even sat next to each other on the bus ride home.

We were so close that when Tayler started passing around invitations to her birthday party, and I *didn't* receive one, it didn't even really cross my mind. I patiently waited until the school day was over, and then I realized I still had not received an invitation even though everyone else in my class was invited. I went over to my friend. Maybe she was just saving the best for last, wanted to invite me *personally.* Well…I was wrong. The response I got from Tayler when I asked her about my invitation was something my 4th grade heart was not prepared to hear, and something I will sadly never forget. She said, "Peter, my mom said I couldn't invite you because you are black."

Wait…what did she say?! Because I am black?! It didn't matter that I was closer to her as a friend than half of the other class members that were invited. I was different, and that made her mom uncomfortable. I decided not to ride the bus that day. I ran home instead. When I got home, I turned on the sink and let the water get as hot as I could. Then I tried to wash the black off of my skin. I didn't want to be different anymore. The next day at school it was all I could notice—I was the only black kid in my class. I started questioning how everyone felt about me. I was different from everyone else, and in my own body I felt like an outcast.

The reality is this is how a lot of minority students feel. They feel like an outcast in spaces where they should be comfortable, simply because they look different, talk different, sound different. According to Dictionary.com, a minority is "a group in society distinguished from, and less dominant than, the more numerous majority." It further says that a minority is, "a racial, ethnic, religious, or social subdivision of a society that is subordinated in political, financial, or social power by the dominant group, without regard to the size of these groups."[1] In other words, a minority is usually a person or group of people that are outnumbered and different from most other people in any culture or situation. Sometimes, tragically and wrongly, minorities are made to feel like they are less than the majority. They often feel like outcasts.

Jesus was a *master* at making outcasts feel included! If you don't believe me, read John chapter 4. In this passage of scripture, Jesus needed to travel from the region of Judea to the region of Galilee. This seems like a simple task, except to most Jews this would be a tricky situation. You see, in order to get from Judea to Galilee you have to pass through the region of Samaria. This was a problem because, in those times, Jews and Samaritans did not get along. They were at odds with each other, especially because of racial tension. The tension was so high that Jews would go *out of their way* when traveling to Galilee to avoid passing through Samaria. Jesus, however, chose not to follow the customs of culture. It says in John 4:4 that *he had to go* through Samaria! Jesus was setting the example for you and I. We love ALL people, and never avoid those that are different from us even if it seems like everyone else is doing it!

Think about what would have happened if Jesus avoided the town of Samaria on that day. Jesus' decision to go through Samaria led to an encounter with a woman at a well, which eventually led to an entire city coming to know Jesus as Lord and Savior! Starting in John 4:6, Jesus sat down at a well and started a conversation with a Samaritan woman who came to get some water. His very willingness to even come near her surprised her. Verse 9 says, "The Samaritan woman said to him, 'You are a Jew and I am a Samaritan woman. How can you ask me for a drink?' (For Jews do not associate with Samaritans)."[2]

The story goes on to tell about Jesus being the living water, and He offered this woman a chance to drink of that water and never thirst again. Jesus went on to tell this woman that he knows all about her past, including the number of husbands she'd had. The woman was amazed and declared in verse 28 "This man knew everything about me...could he be the Messiah?!" The woman returned to her town and told everyone about her encounter with Jesus. Want to know the coolest part? It says in verses 39-41 that because of her testimony *many in her town became believers!* All of this happened because Jesus was willing to love and serve her even though she was different from Him.

Jesus wants ALL people to know him, and wants to use ALL people to spread the good news of the Gospel! But how can ALL know if we avoid those who are different from us? The call for you, a Campus Missionary, goes beyond simple not avoiding people different from you. You are called to *go out of your way* to find those who may feel like they don't belong. When you find them, you are called to bring them into the family of God!

Jesus loves the outcast. He loves those society might push to the side because they are different. Some people in the times of Jesus that were considered outcasts were lepers, those with disabilities, women, slaves, widows, orphans, and the poor. These people were looked down upon by most and treated significantly differently by society, yet these are the people we see Jesus interacting with and loving throughout a majority of his time on earth! In Matthew 8 and Luke 18, Jesus talked with and healed those with leprosy! In Luke 10, Jesus took time to be with Mary and Martha. In Acts 2, Joel's prophecy again proclaimed that the Holy Spirit will be poured out on ALL people—men and women alike!

In John chapter 8, Jesus helped a woman caught in the act of adultery. People from her town were about to stone her to death until Jesus stepped in! He defended her, got down on her level, and forgave her! I would have loved to have been there to see the look on her accusers' faces. Not only was she a sinner, but she was also a woman. To her accusers, she was at the bottom of society, yet she was priceless to Jesus! James 1:27 states, "Religion that God our Father accepts as pure and faultless is this: to look after orphans and widows in their distress…"[3] Finally, in Matthew 25 we see Jesus' heart for the *least of these*. He tells his followers that we must clothe the naked, feed the hungry, visit those in prison, and give shelter to the homeless. Why? Because what we have done unto the *least of these*—those society considered outcasts—we have done unto Jesus.

Treat Every Day Like a Missions Trip

As a Campus Missionary, you must treat every day like you would if you were overseas on the mission field. What do I mean by that? Once you step foot on your school campus it is not a time for you to surround yourself with *your* friends or doing what *you* want. Think about how silly it would be for someone to move to a foreign country to share the Gospel, and then everyday only spend time with the team they went with. Being a missionary means getting to know new people, loving them, and ultimately sharing the Gospel with them! You are on a mission— to seek and save those who are lost. This is the great com*mission*! (Luke 19:10; Matthew 28:16-20). Our job is the great commission, and our means of completing this mission is the great commandment (Mark 12:30-31): Love the Lord your God with all your heart, with all your mind, and with all your soul…and love your neighbor as yourself!

Look for Those Who Are Different

Notice people who are sitting alone at lunch, getting picked on by others, getting chosen last for teams in gym class…and chase them! Don't literally chase them down the hallway, but pursue a friendship with them. Everyone wants to be seen, and you have the eyes of Christ. He will empower you to see people who others seemingly want nothing to do with and show them the love of Christ! Sit with them at lunch, defend them and encourage them when they are being picked on, pick them sooner in gym class. You may be the only one who walks in the doors of your school ready to look for and love those that are different—and you are the perfect person to do that! Be filled up daily with the Holy Spirit. The Holy Spirit will give you the patience, love, and gentleness you need to reach ALL kinds of people and peers.

Invite Them Into Your Life

Remember how Taylor couldn't invite me to her birthday party because I was black? It left a scar on me, and I'll never forget how that discrimination made me feel. I challenge you to do just the opposite. Invite the minority, the outcast, the person who is different into your life. Invite them, not only to church, but to your house. Be a friend to them—which means more than just noticing them. Friends do things together, so invite them and include them in a meaningful way.

Having a Conversation

You may be wondering, "how do I love people who may feel like outcasts because of their differences?" Well, let me ask you this: how would you want to be treated? I know for me, I would want people to learn about me and what makes me unique. Ask questions to genuinely get to know about their culture! Below are some example questions. Don't be afraid to dive in with deep questions when the Holy Spirit prompts you to do so.

- **Where did you grow up? What holidays and traditions do you follow?**
- **What is it like for you being at this school?**
- **How can I be a good friend to you?**
- **How were you raised in terms of faith/religion?**
- **Have you ever been to church or heard about Jesus?**
- **What has been your experience with Christians/Christianity so far?**
- **Would you ever want to come to church with me? What about our campus club?**

---

[1] Dictionary.com, "minority," 2022 Dictionary.com LLC, accessed June 8, 2022.
[2] NIV
[3] NIV

GOD
SO
LOVED....

12

NERDS

Chance Abbott

The nerd is strong with me. I've tried being interested in more culturally acceptable things like sports and fast cars. I've even grown a genuine enjoyment for football over the years, but mostly due to fantasy football leagues. However, the truth is that I hate cars—especially the obnoxiously loud ones. I can't stand basketball (please fix the squeaky shoes), and I find sitting through an entire baseball game a chore. I'm just not that kind of cool. I'm Marvel trading cards, hour-long debates about Batman, and "Ready Player One" on-loop kind of cool.

Today the world is different. Being a nerd is not only acceptable, but in many ways it's a compliment. With a barrage of new MCU and Star Wars shows at the forefront, there has never been a better time to be a nerd! Sci-fi dominates our streaming services, but it wasn't always like this. I remember how hard I had to hide my inner nerd to survive. While everyone else went to various sports practices after school, I rushed home to catch the X-Men cartoons before they started. However, I would have never admitted that to anyone. I hid a sense of shame about the things I enjoyed, and I carried that shame well into adulthood. No one could know that I was a nerd.

I've never forgotten the day when I first felt the weight of this title of "nerd." That was the day I knew it must be kept a secret. It happened during one of those awkward preteen years when you start paying more attention to bands, but also want to keep playing with toys. I was at the park under the playground in the sand with my coveted "Micro Machines Super Van City." Now this toy immediately tells you how old I am, but it was magnificent. It had hills, a working draw bridge, and even a drag strip for racing! Feel free to detour for a quick google search, but don't forget to come back.

Pretty sweet, huh? I was so excited to own that toy. I didn't grow up with a lot of name brands, and the exceptions to that were usually old news by the time I got them. But this was the brand new, official Micro Machines Super Van City and it was mine! So, there I was—in the sand with my poofy red hair and glasses—just being me. Then I saw the cool kid boy (we'll call him Bruce) and cool kid girl (we'll call her Cindy) come walking towards the playground. Something nudged at my mind that I should maybe hide my treasured toys, but I ignored it.

"Maybe Bruce and Cindy will just walk-by. Or maybe they'll even want to see the Super Van! Maybe they'll think it's so cool!" I thought so optimistically. Well…they didn't. I mean they really didn't. Bruce made a mean comment. Then, to my complete surprise, Cindy kicked my city over. Micro Machines flew through the air! Some were forever lost in the sand. But the greatest sting happened as they walked away laughing and Cindy declared, "What a nerd!"

These days on TikTok, someone would call that a villain origin story. I remember feeling a desire for revenge, or some sort of justice. Truthfully though, I mostly remember how much it hurt my feelings; how insignificant it made me feel…how small it made me feel. I liked nerdy things and admittedly I was a bit of dork, but in that moment, I felt great shame and wanted to hide. I felt powerless. Those feelings, and that experience, are things us nerds often share.

Have you ever noticed how much work we put into maintaining a particular image? Reputation is a big deal. Maintaining a reputation involves a lot of highlighting key areas of life, and intentionally keeping other areas of life hidden. Today, it's common knowledge that most people have online, somewhat misleading public personas. We've been doing the same thing in real life for generations—presenting the public with the parts of us we want to be seen, while hiding the parts we find embarrassing.

Ironically, we live in a culture that falsely states "be true to yourself." Even more so are the constant reminders of being the "real you" in every superhero storyline. As much as we love our heroes, we still struggle to put this into practice. Somewhere along the way we stopped being ourselves in order to please others. We often pretend to be someone we're not. It isn't to save the world, it's to save ourselves from pain. Vulnerability is the shared kryptonite of nerds, jocks, hipsters, mean-girls and scenesters.

Reaching people with the Gospel requires meeting them where they are and loving them as they are—the real them, hidden parts and all. This is what Jesus did. That doesn't mean we have to be like them or even agree with them. It doesn't mean we accept of affirm obvious sin issues in their lives. It simply means we acknowledge them where they're at, and we love them because they, like us, are created in God's image.

There's a story from Luke's Gospel about a tax collector named Zacchaeus. This story is most often taught to children, but if we are honest, it is probably far more applicable to adults. One of the few details we are given about Zacchaeus is that he's a tax collector, which means most people hated him. He was a wealthy tax collector, which means most people probably had good reason to hate him. And he was short. This is where the kids' songs and cartoon imagery come in. So, what does a short person without any real friends do when Jesus is walking through the crowd? He climbs a tree to catch a glimpse. Kind of a dorky thing to do. A short, grown man (that's balding in the cartoons for some reason) in a dress-like Bible robe climbs a tree and quietly watches. He wasn't trying to strike up a conversation, but a good conversation finds him.

"When Jesus came by, he looked up at Zacchaeus and called him by name. 'Zacchaeus!' he said. 'Quick, come down! I must be a guest in your home today.'"[1]

Secret Handshake BFF Treatment

Jesus was looking. That's step one. If you're reading this book that means you're probably looking too. Looking for the lost. Looking for those that need the hope of Jesus. We see pain and hurt in the world with ease; it's all over the place. While we see the hurt, we won't really see the hurting unless we're looking. After Jesus sees Zacchaeus, He calls Zacchaeus by name. Jesus, in front of all those people, called out Zacchaeus as if he were an old friend. Jesus didn't seem one bit ashamed to know who Zacchaeus was. I think my favorite part is when Jesus invites himself over. That took their social relationship to a new level.

Jesus gave Zacchaeus the secret handshake, BFF treatment. No embarrassment. No shame. How did Zacchaeus respond to such an affirming exchange? "Zacchaeus quickly climbed down and took Jesus to his house in great excitement and joy."[2] If you want to share Jesus with the nerds in your life, don't just love them—like them! Give them the secret handshake, BFF treatment.

Talk Nerdy to Me

You know what nerds love to do? Talk about nerdy things. If you show the slightest interest in lightsabers, odds are the word "kyber" is about to come out of my mouth. If you so much as mention Galaxy's Edge, we're either about to be great friends or you're going to regret meeting me. If there's one thing I have almost no restraint in, it's talking about the things I'm excited about, and if show me you have genuine interest—let's go! One key to reaching nerds is showing interest. They love to talk about it. For nerds, explaining nerds things is like having an itch they can't help but scratch.

Jesus showed an interest in Zacchaeus. He answered Zacchaeus' question. If you want to earn the right to share Jesus with a nerd, talk nerdy to him or her. You'll be amazed at how much they appreciate being heard.

22-Minutes or More

I've become an advocate for 22-minute conversations. This is about the same length as the runtime of most "half hour" shows once you include commercials or ads. It's short enough that it doesn't feel like a big commitment, but long enough to push past some of the small talk fluff. I think you'd be amazed what a 22-minute conversation without distractions will do for any relationship you have. The challenge you'll find with nerds is that once you break the ice, they're likely to run off into the depths and details for the next 45 minutes. So be prepared for a few long conversations.

Jesus settled in for the long haul in his conversations with Zacchaeus. Jesus went to his house! He was ready to take more time with Zacchaeus than with the rest of the crowd. What was the result? Zacchaeus was transformed. Not only did Zacchaeus wholeheartedly apologize for taking advantage of people, but he also offered to pay back what he had taken times four. The crowd scoffed at Jesus for going to with Zacchaeus, but Zacchaeus and his entire home found hope and healing.

Having a Conversation

If you're a nerd like me, you may not need help having great conversations with another nerd. If you're not sure what questions to ask to get a conversation started, try these:

- **Who's your favorite hero? What about their story or powers interests you?** It's easy to list out a favorite superhero or two. Knowing why that superhero is a favorite can be telling. Many of us like heroes that we feel we share character traits with.

- **Who are some of your favorite characters?** This can open up conversations from Harry Potter to Rey Skywalker. So many of these stories are easy to connect with because they are about someone being significant in some way. Often the most unlikely characters become fan favorites. Everyone wants to feel like they matter and Jesus gives us more worth than we could possibly imagine.

- **What character origin story is your favorite?** Our culture is obsessed with origin stories. We don't just want to know the character; we want to know why they are the way that they are. Origin stories highlight significant moments of life change. This can start a conversation about big moments in real life.

- **What is your origin story? In what way do you think God wants to be a part of it?** Listen to what your friend has to say about his or her origin. Ask the Holy Spirit to help you see where God has been moving your friend's life and talk about it with him or her.

- **What do you think about Jesus' origin story? What are characteristics of Jesus do you like most?** Many superhero stories are actually influenced by Jesus' story; they often sacrifice their own life to save others. Jesus is the original sacrificial hero. Point these similarities out and invite your friend to know this hero.

---

[1] Luke 19:5 NLT
[2] Luke 19:6 NLT

GOD
SO
LOVED....

<u>13</u>

THE NEW KID AT SCHOOL

Billy Willis

"Hey, would you like to come sit with us?" Those words carry incredible weight in my heart because they were the words that brought relief and hope when I was the new kid in Middle School. In the middle of eighth grade, my family and I moved to Illinois from Florida. Let me give you a little background; my dad was in the military so we moved around A LOT. Moving to Illinois was at least the twelfth time my family moved into a new home, the sixth time we moved to a new state, and the seventh time I was the "new kid" at school—all before my 15th birthday.

Sometimes moving was exciting, giving me the opportunity to get a fresh start and live in cool places like Florida. Sometimes moving was devastating and disruptive. Those two words capture how I felt about the move from Florida to Illinois. In Florida I had my own bedroom, a big backyard with a rope swing, a trampoline, and a tree house that my dad built for my 12th birthday. I had a best friend and a group of friends at school. I had my own cat and a dog that slept by my side every night. I was even part of a youth group and was just starting to really learn about Jesus. I was getting settled in for the first time in my life when one day my parents told me that we were moving AGAIN, this time to Illinois.

We were moving away from warm weather to cold weather. It was wintertime, and I was not going to be able to skateboard or ride my bike for several more months until all the snow melted in Spring. We were moving out of our own house to move in with my grandpa in a smaller house with no yard. I was going to have to get rid of my cat and dog. My best friend was going to be close to a thousand miles away. I was going to be the "new kid" one more time. I still remember going to bed one night after the move. My face was drenched in tears and my mouth gasping for breath as I cried myself to sleep feeling lonely, displaced, and fearful of being the new kid at school.

My first experience at my new school was not pleasant or exciting at all. On my first day of school, kids in every class were curious about the new kid and wanted to know where I moved from. When I told them that I moved from Florida, they would awkwardly look at me like I was crazy ask, "Why in the world would you move from Florida to Illinois?" The tone they used caused me to feel ashamed, stupid, and it only magnified the pain of moving. I didn't know how to respond. It's not like I chose to move; it was my parents' decision, and I was suffering for it.

I was shy and paralyzed with fear of doing anything that would cause people not to like me. My new classmates, on the other hand, had their own reputation to maintain and were not quick to make friends with the new kid at school until they were able to successfully figure out which social group I fit into. They looked at the way I dressed, how I wore my hair, and what brand of shoes I wore. Honestly, I didn't know what I was or what social group I belonged to anymore. All I knew is that I used to belong to a group of friends that was now 971 miles away. Now I had no friends and I felt alone in a new school. I was desperate for a place to belong.

Having new classes was challenging enough, but lunch felt the scariest. Step into the shoes of the new kid at your school. You walk into the lunch room for the first time. It's the largest, loudest, and most crowded room you've been in so far. It's very intimidating. You locate the lunch line and you file in. After you make your way through the line, with food in hand, you awkwardly pause to scope out the room in hopes of seeing a friend to sit next to, only to remember that you have no friends here. You are alone, so you nervously scurry to an empty table and sit down to eat lunch by yourself. There is no one to talk to, no one to joke around with, and no one to share food with. That's where I found myself the first day of school at lunch time. I was terribly alone.

I began to nervously eat my food, fighting back the tears associated with being alone. Then, I heard the voice of a teenage boy utter the words, "Hey, would you like to come sit with us?" Those words brought hope to a hopeless moment. Careful not to show my relief or excitement, I played it cool and obliged. I proceeded to walk with him to the table and sit with him and his group of friends. For the first time, I didn't feel alone. I was welcome here. Most of his friends at this table were of second generation Mexican-Americans. I had very little in common with them. I was a tall, gangly, pasty white kid with a southern accent and minimal exposure to Mexican-American culture, yet I sat with this group every day the rest of my 8th grade year because that was where I felt welcome. That kid who invited me to sit at his table with his friends—his name was Nick. I will never forget his name because he was the first kid at my new school to make me feel welcome. It was one of the nicest thing anyone has ever done for me.

Nick showed compassion for me. Compassion happens when we feel kindness and love and it moves us to take action to help someone or fix a problem. In other words, compassion allows us to step into another person's shoes, to feel what they feel, and to do something about it. Jesus had compassion. We see this in Matthew 9:36, "When he saw the crowds, he had compassion on them because they were confused and helpless, like sheep without a shepherd." Jesus wants us to reach the new kid at school, not out of guilt or obligation, but because it's what He would do. He wants us to be compelled by love and act with compassion. I often ask the Lord, "Give me your eyes today. Help me to see people the way that you do, and just as your love for them compelled you to die on the cross, help me to love them in a way that will compel me to take action and do something to shine the light of your love to them." I challenge you to pray something like that each day. When we feel genuine compassion for the new kid at school, or anyone for that matter, it should move us to action.

Invite Them Into Your Lunch Table

Reaching the new kids at school can start with something as simple as what Nick did for me by inviting them to sit with you at lunch. When you do, you might be doing one of the nicest things anyone has ever done for them. They might even recall what you did for them 20 years from now and explain how it ultimately led them to Jesus. Imagine them telling their story some day! "I have a relationship with Jesus and I'm going to heaven because _____ (insert your name) reached out to me when I was the new kid at school." That would be amazing! When lunch is over and it's time to get to class, be sure to reassure them that you really enjoyed eating lunch together and getting to know them a little bit. Invite them to sit with you again the next day. If you cross paths in the hallway, greet them by name with a smile as you reach up to give them a high-five or a fist bump.

Invite Them Into Your Life

Lunch is not the only time the new kids at school need a friend. If they are new to the school, they are probably also new to the area. So they may not have any friends at all. Get their phone number and their social media information too, that way you have another way of connecting with them outside of school. Show them that you genuinely care about them as a person by inviting them to be your friend all around, not just at lunch. You can do that by simply asking them to share their story and ask them questions about their life and their interests. Invite them to your house, to some of the activities you're involved with, or just to hang out together. Work together with some of your youth group friends to make the new kid feel welcome. Let the first and best social group the new kids hang out with be the Christian students at school!

Invite Them Into Your Youth Group

If you're building a genuine friendship with the new kid at school, it will only be natural that you eventually invite them to church. When you're friends with someone, you get to know their interests, and church or youth group is one of your interests! Don't hide it, instead be authentic by inviting your new friend so something that is so important to you. In your new friendship, you may not have the opportunity to switch gears and talk about Jesus initially, and that is okay. Just don't lose sight that sharing Jesus is what you are ultimately called by God to do. Church or youth group is a great social situation to invite the new kid into in the meantime—a place they will be welcomed and also hear about God. Inviting the new kid is a great way to move in the direction of talking to them about Jesus. If you were there when I was the new kid at school and invited me to youth group, I would have gone with you in a heartbeat!

Having the Conversation

Starting a conversation with someone you never met before can be intimidating. Here are some questions and conversation starters to get you going:

- **"Tell me about yourself."** Take a genuine interest in the new kid! Not only does this show that you care, you will also make a new friend!

- **"How has moving to the area been?"** Ask him what's going on outside school and how he is holding up. New kids are going through some big changes and could use a friend to listen to their challenges.

- **"Have you met, (insert name of other Christian friends name)?"** The goal is to connect your other Christian friends with the new kid. Keep in mind that not everyone connects well. There will be times where you are two polar opposites, so connecting them to more Christians helps broaden the opportunities for great relationships.

- **"How are you?"** This is simple, but if you take the time to really listen, it can be so powerful. It's especially helpful to the new kid—it means a lot that anyone would ask. Make sure you are just loving in every part of this conversation and be ready for some sad or happy thoughts from the new kid.

- **"Hey, is it cool if I keep you in my prayers?"** This question opens a lot of doors. It lets the new kid that you pray and you're probably a Christian. It lets him or her know that you care enough to pray for them, and are polite enough to ask them for their permission. Of course, you don't actually need their permission to pray for the new kid, but this a great question because it opens up a dialogue of care and faith. Plus, praying is a great thing to do!

GOD SO LOVED....

14

OUTDOORSMEN

Kris Lewis

If you own a homemade fur coat, you might be a redneck.

If you've ever filled your deer tag on the golf course, you might be a redneck.

If the primary color of your car is bondo, you might be a redneck.

If you come back from the garbage dump with more than what you took to it, you might be a redneck.

—*Jeff Foxworthy*

"Hunters! Fisherman! Rednecks! Lend me your deers!" If there were ever a group of people ready to be told about Jesus, it would be the hunting, fishing, and general outdoors group. Oftentimes they are referred to as "rednecks" in a derogatory manner, but these are some amazing people!

I grew up and live among people who think the first day of deer season should be a national holiday. Men and women save up their vacation time—it really is a big deal for us! In Pennsylvania in 2014, there were 943,000 hunting licenses sold![1] We call all of these hunters "The Orange Army," because hunters are required to wear fluorescent orange. If it really were an army, the hunters in Pennsylvania alone would be the 5th largest army in the world![2] It's a big part of our culture. In the late fall every year, The Orange Army takes to the woods to fill those deer tags. We take our hunting and fishing seriously around these parts!

More importantly, A LOT of teenagers like to hunt, and many also enjoy fishing and other parts of the outdoors. So many students

99

take off for hunting season that schools often close because it's impossible to have class with so many missing. In my state, more than 120,000 teenagers got hunting licenses last season.[3] It's not just a huge part of our culture; it's a huge part of their identities. God so loved the outdoorsman, and so should you.

If you have never taken to the woods, or held a fishing pole, you probably aren't a redneck! But I bet you've seen a few in your school, and they need to know about the love of Jesus too. Honestly, many people in this group are already part of a church in some form—maybe they go to church on special occasions, or their family prays during a holiday meal. The fact is, most rednecks have some level of appreciation for church, spirituality, and religion. But just like other groups, many have never experienced what a relationship with Jesus can do for them.

When I was in school, when a guy or girl came of age to get a vehicle, it became clear how much "red" was in their blood. If their first vehicle was a Toyota Camry or a Honda Civic, they probably weren't a part of this group. You could spot a redneck a mile away. Their vehicle of choice was a jacked up 4x4 truck, the kind you might even see at a monster truck rally! In fact I'm pretty sure one of the guys from my high school tried to drive over small cars with his truck!

If that didn't show you how "red" their blood was, you could always check out their choice of footwear. If they wore heavy outdoor boots more often then any other type of shoe, they might have been a redneck. And if that didn't set you off, you could always listen to their vocabulary. There's a certain amount of slang in a redneck's vocab.

> Allure: *n.* an object used for enticement, with the intention of capturing prey. "You want to catch a fish, you gotta use allure."
>
> Cauterize: v and n. to visually engage a female person's ocular organs. "It was love at first sight the second I cauterize."
>
> County: v and n. to combine integers, as done by a male person. "To county has to take off his shoes, if you want him to get past ten."
>
> Paranormal: n and adj. two things or persons representative of the mean or otherwise average. "Don't pay any attention to them, Jane, I think you've got a paranormal kids."
>
> —Jeff Foxworthy, *Redneck Dictionary 2*

That's fun—I don't care who you are! And the best part is that some of this stuff is actually true. Many hunters, fishers, or outdoorsmen actually talk with a level of slurring or slang words. But in all honestly, many people who speak clearly and don't have 4-5 broken down cars in their front yard are actually a part of this group, too. There are people who have high level corporate jobs that are regulars to the woods and the boat. The fundamental connection that all of these people have is a love and respect for the outdoors.

I recently had a conversation with my brother-in-law about his love for Creation. He told me that when he is outdoors he finds that he tends to just stop and look in awe at the level of beauty in nature. The Bible talks about how the beauty of nature points towards God's majesty. Psalm 19:1-4 says, "The heavens declare the glory of God; the skies proclaim the work of his hands. Day after day they pour forth speech; night after night they display knowledge. There is no speech or language where their voice is not heard. Their voice goes out into all the earth, their words to the ends of the world."[4] Hunters, fishers, and outdoorsy people always seem to have an appreciation for the Creation they are wandering about.

An old college friend of mine shared how he likes to escape into the world of fishing and hunting. Escape is a key word. The world travels so fast around us, and when a person escapes to the outdoors, it's as if life slows down. When I was a student I personally didn't understand this. It wasn't till I got married, had kids, and had a number of years under my belt as a busy youth pastor that I realized the draw of the outdoors. Even getting up at 4am and heading out to my tree stand, exhausted, was relaxing and refreshing.

Ask About Their Stories

As you seek to engage outdoorsmen with conversation, here is a good tip: they love to tell stories about their outdoor adventures. This is a great way to get to know them better, and it will demonstrate that you have a genuine interest in them! The Gospel is best shared through friendship, and you can't have friendship without conversation, so ask them about their adventures and get them talking! Here's another tip if you want to talk with a hunter: mention deer... that's pretty much all you need! Get a hunter talking about their time in the woods, especially if its during the season at the time (usually in the fall). If it's a person who loves fishing, ask about their favorite spot to fish, or about "the one that got away." Ask how their experiences have been this year. Get them to tell you stories! That is a great way to build a relationship. Remember "people don't care how much you know until they know how much you care."[5] If you show that you actually care about them as a person, you are much further down the road to sharing Jesus with them.

Go Hunting...or Fishing...or Hiking

Another way that could lend itself to building a relationship, if you are serious, is to ask your friend to take you fishing, hunting, or to show you around their favorite spots in the outdoors. Skilled outdoorsmen love to share their experiences with others! What better opportunity to share Jesus with someone than when you're in a boat together in the middle of the lake? Talk about a captive audience! Remember, even Jesus went fishing with his disciples, and he himself was not a fisherman, but a carpenter.[6]

Have a Party

If you wanted to do something as a Bible Club to reach out to hunters and fishers in your school, try hosting a special party or service for them. Play a fishing game with a kiddy pool, or use Nerf guns and setup a target range with fake deer (if school policy allows this). Talk with your youth pastor or prepare to share a lesson that connects the love of the created world with the greatness of God. Invite all the hunters to a special prayer or blessing over them just before the main hunting season. Pray for their safety and for their success. Share how God isn't just the Creator; He also desires to have a relationship with us as people! Deck the place out in camo and blaze orange! Rednecks can't get enough of that!

Having a Conversation

Here are a few ideas for conversation starters or talking points:

- **Did you hunt this year? What was the most exciting part?**
- **How did you get started hunting?**
- **Have you been fishing lately? How has it gone? What has been the best part?**
- **I've never gotten into fishing, but I'm interested in it. Where should I start?**

- What draws you into nature? What is your favorite part of being there? What makes it your favorite?

- I've heard about something people call "buck fever"— when you are about to shoot a deer and your adrenaline gets all amped up and you get all shaky. Has that happened to you? What was it like?

- There is something primal about hunting/fishing; something almost spiritual in nature to it. I've heard of how some guys when they hunt, fish or just out in nature, they feel closer to God. Have you ever thought about God when you are out in the woods? What do you think about God? What does nature teach you about Him?

- I believe God is real and that He created all of nature. What do you believe? Do you think that the world was created on purpose or was it some sort of accident?

---

[1] Pennsylvania Game Commission, "Hunting License Sales Report," http://www.portal.state.pa.us/portal/server.pt?open=514&objID=596054&mode =2 (accessed February 3, 2016).

[2] World Atlas, "29 Largest Armies in the World," World Facts, http://www.worldatlas.com/articles/29-largest-armies-in-the-world.html (accessed February 3, 2016).

[3] Pennsylvania Game Commission.

[4] NIV 1984.

[5] No one seems to be sure who originally said this, but it is widely credited to both former president Theodore Roosevelt and leadership expert John Maxwell.

[6] Luke 5:1-11.

GOD
SO
LOVED....

15

QUIET STUDENTS

Joe Cali

single most dreaded day of the year which I had hoped would never come. On this day in English class, we had to present a book report. This meant that every student had to stand up in front of the class, one by one, and share what their book was all about. I had feared this moment. Just the thought of me standing in front of other students and speaking was making me sweat.

As a quiet middle schooler, I just sat in the class trying to avoid eye-contact with my teacher. I knew if I made eye-contact she would pick me next. I sat there hoping and praying that she wouldn't call out my name. Just maybe, she would overlook me. To be honest, the rest of my peers also constantly avoided eye-contact. I often thought to myself, "If I die would anyone come to my funeral? Would anyone ever notice if Joe was no longer with us?" Maybe my teacher would forget about me and move on to the other students in my class. Then, to my disappointment, she called out my name.

"Joe Cali, you're up!"

My palms were sweaty. My hands were shaking. I couldn't keep my knees from knocking, swaying back and forth, and *especially* making no eye contact with anyone. In my mind I was telling myself, "I can't wait until this is over."

Speaking in front of my peers, publicly was the last thing I wanted to do. All throughout my elementary and middle school years I was known as the quiet student. Not many people bothered with me. I wasn't the class clown. I wasn't the most popular. I wasn't the first person people wanted to pick for sports. I felt like I was always overlooked and unnoticed. Don't get me wrong—I never felt hated. It was more like people didn't want to bother with me. They were okay with me being around because I would smile or laugh a lot, but I never felt accepted.

As a quiet student, I didn't really talk much to others. It wasn't because I didn't want to talk or I didn't like to talk to other people. I wanted to have some friendships. I really did want to talk to others. I just never knew how to start the conversation with someone, or I figured people didn't like me so I'll just keep to myself. Oftentimes, the only reason people wanted me around was because I would laugh at their jokes or sayings.

Stop for a moment and think about your school. Picture your classes, your lunch room, and the bus ride. Can you see the quiet students? Can you see them sitting quietly, not having many conversations? Can you see them secluded, often alone? The quiet students are often found alone and sticking to themselves. Most outgoing students don't talk with them or don't even bother with them. These quiet students aren't making eye contact with others as they sit in class or as they ride the bus. They are often overlooked or unnoticed. They may just be waiting for a follower of Jesus, a Campus Missionary like you, to notice them and talk to them.

In the book of Luke there is an account of a short man named Zacchaeus. Zacchaeus was a chief tax collector in his town. He was severely disliked by the townspeople, in part because most people don't like to pay taxes. We find out in Luke 19 that Zacchaeus would often charge people more than he should for taxes as well, causing more people to not want him around. He was most likely not included in many friend-groups. He most likely learned to keep to himself and found himself often alone. He probably wasn't invited to hang out with many people.

One day, however, Zacchaeus life changed. Zacchaeus heard the news that Jesus was walking through his town that day. He had heard about this man named Jesus and knew he just had to see Him. Since he was a short man, he decided to climb up a sycamore tree so he can get his eyes on Jesus. As Jesus was walking by, He stopped and noticed that there was a man in the tree.

When Jesus reached the spot, he looked up and said to him, "Zacchaeus, come down immediately. I must stay at your house

today." So he came down at once and welcomed him gladly. 7 All
the people saw this and began to mutter, "He has gone to be the
guest of a sinner." But Zacchaeus stood up and said to the Lord,
"Look, Lord! Here and now I give half of my possessions to the
poor, and if I have cheated anybody out of anything, I will pay
back four times the amount." Jesus said to him, "Today salvation
has come to this house, because this man, too, is a son of
Abraham. For the Son of Man came to seek and to save the lost.
Luke 19:5-10 NIV

Jesus looked up and noticed Zacchaeus in the tree. He stopped and called out to him by name, "Zacchaeus!" This made Zacchaeus' day! Jesus hung out with Zacchaeus, and we see this made a dramatic impact on not just Zacchaeus life, but his entire household. God saw Zacchaeus.

It wasn't until my high school years when I finally realized that God saw me. God knew who I was. God knew I was a quiet person, and God was okay with that. When I realized what Jesus did for me and who I was in Christ, I decided to make a declaration to God. I declared that I was going to follow Him no matter who else was—or was not—following Him. I adopted an attitude that said, "I don't care what others think about me or God, I'm going to serve Him."

This was a posture I started to hold because I knew I might lose friendships or relationships over the Scriptural standards I began to follow. I was determined to keep my relationship with my Creator, God Himself. That was the moment I began to realize I couldn't be quiet anymore. It was like I finally could talk and not be as nervous. I realized people *did like* to talk with me. It had all just been in my head. Truly, if I wanted to keep God first and live for Him, I need to start stepping out and telling people all about Jesus.

I began to look around in my school and my job and try to find other quiet students. I would hype myself up before walking over to them because it was out of my natural character to do so. I knew these quiet students would welcome a conversation. If I could just strike up a conversation with them, they would see that I had noticed them. If I noticed them, then just maybe I can let them know I care about them. If I care about them, then I would really try to point them to Jesus.

As a student on a school campus, or when you are around

other teenagers, I encourage you to slow down and look around. Who can you identify as a student who is quiet? God sent Jesus to die for all people, even the quiet students. It's important to look around and notice those students who are quiet. These are the students that will come alive if and when you give them attention. They most likely will join you for anything you ask them to be a part of. Take the first step walk over and then initiate a conversation with them. Remember, Jesus walked the street and noticed Zacchaeus. Jesus started his conversation with Zacchaeus by calling him by name and then creating an opportunity to hang out with him.

Imagine if you were the one to help the quiet student realize who they can be in Christ. What if the quiet student began to talk more and became more confident because you were able to connect them with the one who created them? Why not help them develop a relationship with Jesus Christ?

Notice and Take Initiative

At times it might seem like quiet students don't want to be bothered, or that they are rude and think that they are better than you. However, this is usually not the case. It's likely they are just waiting for someone to notice them. Maybe they are too embarrassed, afraid, or lack the self-esteem to even look up and try to strike up a conversation. God created every individual with various personalities and character traits. The quiet students are not just quiet because they are weird or they can't talk. Quiet students might sit alone because they are too shy to talk. Quiet students might hold themselves in an awkward way because they don't think anyone notices them. You can serve the quiet students in your life by noticing them and taking the initiative to go to them. Talk with them. Find out more about them. Discover what would make them more comfortable or what they are interested in. Let them know you notice them and you care about them.

Strike Up A Conversation

Most quiet students will not begin a conversation on their own unless they are forced to, and when they are forced to they won't enjoy it. Instead, ease the burden on them by starting the conversation yourself. After all, if your goal is to share the Gospel, you are going to have to start a conversation to make that happen. Use the questions at the end of this chapter to start a conversation. Remember, your goal isn't to make a quiet student less quiet, it's to share Jesus with them. God loves the quiet student just they are, and so should you. It's okay if they remain quiet even after they accept Jesus—God will use their quietness just like God is using your abilities. Remember, quiet students often long for meaningful friendships, so don't just have one conversation. Instead, make it your goal to have several conversations within a week or two as a way of starting a friendship.

Invite Them to Join You

Once you've struck up a friendship, invite your new quiet friend into your life by inviting them to do things with you. It can be as simple as running an errand together. At some point, you should definitely invite them to church with you. Relationships start with a conversation, and they are made stronger by experiencing and doing things together. This is what Jesus did with the disciples, so do this with the quiet friends in your life.

Having a Conversation

Use these questions and pointers to start a conversation with the quiet students around you:

- **Hey how's it going? My name is _____ what's yours?**
- **Give a compliment like, "I like your shoes."** Everyone likes to be complimented, so maybe start with that as an ice-breaker to having conversation.
- **I noticed you over here and I was wondering if you want to hang out?**
- **What do you like to do for fun? Tell me about that.**
- **Invite your quiet friend to hang out with you at your church or youth group.**

GOD
SO
LOVED....

<u>16</u>

SPECIAL NEEDS STUDENTS

Grayson Wade

When I think about my first day of middle school, I can still feel the mix of excitement and anxiety. While I was excited to meet new friends, I was also afraid of the unknown. Starting at a new school meant starting over, and I wasn't sure how well I would adjust. In the town where I grew up, there were seven elementary schools. Each school was made up of students from a small geographical area. That meant that the majority of people I went to school with either lived in my neighborhood or another neighborhood nearby. This proximity created a sense of comfort and familiarity. I knew everyone in my school because we had been neighbors, classmates, and teammates for years.

When it came time for middle school, the closeness and familiarity I had felt changed. Students from all seven elementary schools were brought together. Suddenly, I didn't know everyone. I was afraid I wouldn't be able to find my place in a school that was much bigger than what I was used to. Ultimately, I had my concerns but I knew that I would be okay. Even if it took a while to make new friends, I felt like I could figure it out. While I did not worry too much about myself, I did worry about my friend David.

111

David and I grew up going to the same elementary school. Over the years, we had built a strong friendship. Even though David was autistic, it never felt like he was out of place. Many of the students at our school went out of their way to make him feel included in whatever they were doing. Much of this was possible because we had all known David for years. I was worried that he would not receive the same welcome at our new middle school.

Change can be difficult for students with special needs. While all of us naturally have reservations when it comes to new experiences, these feelings are amplified with special needs students. I worried about David because I knew that a new environment would be incredibly overwhelming for him. I was also concerned about how he would be received by students who did not know him.

There is a passage in Luke that *The Message* labels, "Invite the Misfits." In this passage, Jesus talks about ministering to those who are overlooked. It says, "The next time you put on a dinner, don't just invite your friends and family and rich neighbors, the kind of people who will return the favor. Invite some people who never get invited out, the misfits from the wrong side of the tracks. You'll be—and experience—a blessing. They won't be able to return the favor, but the favor will be returned—oh, how it will be returned!—at the resurrection of God's people" (Luke 14:12b-14 MSG).

If you were getting a group of people together to hang out, who would you invite? Close friends and family would probably be at the top of the list. Then, you may invite someone that sits at a more popular lunch table than the one you sit at. The rationale is that your friends will invite you over the next time that they get together, and hopefully your more popular friend will help you get connected with new friends. In this scenario, everyone that you invite can in some way repay you.

Jesus pushes back against this mindset when He says the next time you get a group together, "invite some people who never get invited out." While talking about the overlooked, I believe that He is saying that part of true ministry is loving people who can never repay you. When we minister to people who can repay us, there are benefits that we will see here on Earth. When we minister to people who cannot repay us, people who never get invited out, we get something better- benefits in Heaven.

Today, my friend group looks nothing like it did in middle school and high school. Almost every friendship that I had fizzled away due to time and distance. One of the few exceptions is my friend James. This friendship is unique because it did not form naturally.

My first interaction with James came in math class. When we met, we did not like each other. After a few short conversations in class, we realized that we had almost nothing in common. Consistently, if I believed something, James believed the exact opposite. Over time, James and I had more conversations, and somewhere along the way we became friends. This friendship did not form naturally because of a shared interest. It formed because we made an effort to understand one another.

Too often we settle for easy relationships. We surround ourselves with people who believe, talk, and dress like we do. Jesus' call to minister to the overlooked shows us that some of the most meaningful relationships in our lives come from people that we don't naturally connect with. When we choose to minister to people outside of our comfort zone, God does something that reaches beyond our current reality and into eternity.

Special needs students are worth our time. In most cases, these relationships will not come naturally. They require us to make an effort to find common ground, include, and celebrate students with disabilities. If Jesus' call tells us anything, it tells us that this effort will yield eternal results.

Find Common Ground

Most students have multiple interests. They may participate in more than one extracurricular activity and have a variety of subjects that they are passionate about. For many special needs students, they are devoted to a smaller number of hobbies or interests. Whether it be movies, sports, art, or video games, they are often more devoted than the average student. Starting a conversation about these interests is a great way to connect. Once the student starts to talk about what they love, find a way to connect it back to your own interests. You may have more in common than you think.

Include

One of my pet peeves is sitting at a table where everyone is having a conversation and one person is left out. When I find myself in these situations, I will go out of my way to explain the conversation to the person who is not being included. If the conversation continues to leave him or her left out, I will try to find ways to pull that one person back in. An easy way to do this is by finding common ground. If someone is not being included in the conversation, try to find ways that he or she can connect to the conversation. Then, ask questions that help make him or her a part of what is going on.

One of the most effective ways to reach special needs students is including them in what you do. If you eat lunch with the same group every day, invite them to come sit with you. If you have a Bible club at your school, invite them to go with you. Often times, a simple invitation will go a long way in showing that you care. Keep in mind, you will probably have to do more than just extend an invitation. Once you include special needs students in whatever you are doing, you will have to make an effort to make sure that they are a part of the conversation.

Celebrate

Earlier I shared my concerns about how my friend David would be received in middle school. Thankfully, when we got to our new school, we were placed on the same academic team. We had the same classes and got to see each other multiple times a day. A few months into the school year, David got really into drawing cartoon characters. In a short amount of time, he got really good at it.

When I noticed that David was drawing a lot, I asked him to draw me a character. When he finished the drawing, I made a big deal out of it and displayed it in my locker. Every time I opened my locker, people would see David's drawing. Over the next few weeks, people started asking David to draw a character for them. It didn't take long before many students on our academic team had one of David's drawings in their locker. This was a great way to celebrate him and also help him feel welcome and included at a new school.

Having a Conversation

As you work towards finding common ground and including your special needs friend, use these discussion questions to have a great conversation:

- **What do you like to do?** This is an easy way to find common ground with a special needs student. When they open up and begin to share their interests, be sure to keep asking questions. You can show that you care by being interested in what they are interested in. This simple question will help open the door.

- **Would you like to eat lunch with me?** In many cases, lunch at school is a time when students can feel disconnected. Inviting a special needs student to eat lunch with you is a great way to help them feel included. Remember, when you do invite them to be a part, be sure to include them in the conversation once they join you.

- **Ask an aide: How can I be a better friend to ____?** Many special needs students while have an aide that travels with them from class to class. Often, the aide will be able to give you ideas on how to serve their student. In my case, reaching out to my friend David's aide helped me reach David in a more effective way.

- **What do you think Jesus says about you?** This is a great question to ask that will give you an opportunity to let your special needs friend know how much God loves them. If and when you ask this question, be sure to be ready with the right answers. Share some Scriptures about God's love for your friend, and be sure to let them know that you love them too.

GOD
SO
LOVED....

17

THE UNDERPRIVILEGED

John Ginnan

Jason, an eighth-grader, was well liked at the teen center. He loved hanging out there each afternoon partly because they had free food, and partly because it was a fun and safe place to be for him and his friends. Jason's mom was very caring and involved in his life, but she also worked two jobs just to pay the bills. His dad lived out of state. Jason never had the funds to go on any trips with the teen center, and this always made him disappointed. However, the caring adult staff from the teen center could usually find ways to sponsor his trips. Many times they would even let Jason take the leftover teen center food home with him. But as he spent time with others he was constantly reminded of his underprivileged status.

Jason had a buddy named Brian. Brian lived with his mom and her boyfriend, who was an alcohol-abusing and drug-addicted man. Both Jason and Brian got a lot out of going to the teen center. They were always together, either at school or in the neighborhood. Jason and Brian enjoyed similar movies, video games, picking up energy drinks at the convenience store, and of course, dropping by the teen center.

As summer passed and eighth grade gave way to ninth, one of Brian's friends introduced him to marijuana. Brian gave in, and started down a path that led him into selling drugs. Through money collected from drug dealing, it wasn't long before Brian's life had made a dramatic shift. With his new illegal and risky occupation, he had gone from having nothing to suddenly being able to buy nearly anything he had ever wanted. But as a consequence of Brian's new and very busy life path, Jason grew distant from him. Soon Jason felt like he didn't have anyone who really understood him.

Camryn, a high school junior, was starting a Christian club at her school. It had been a dream of hers to encourage her friends to know Jesus through an after-school ministry. Her friend Andy, a junior as well, was her club co-leader. Andy often came to the teen center to share Jesus with the students there. This year Andy had been having a few conversations with Jason about Jesus.

Andy invited Jason to the Christian club's big launch party, adding, "It's gonna be a lot of fun, and there'll be free pizza for everyone!" Jason wouldn't pass up the opportunity for free food.

Soon the Christian club's launch day had arrived! Camryn & Andy's plan was in big letters on the white board of their Math teacher's classroom, whom Andy knew from his church. It read: "Plan:" followed by, "People, Pizza, Playing a game & Purpose of our new club." Moments from the start bell of the after school period, in came Jason.

"Hey–you made it!" said Andy.

Jason quietly headed to a table where three pizzas were laid out, stacked three slices on his tiny plate and sat down away from the rest of the group. None of the students in the club were Jason's friends. As the club activities were underway, Jason sat wondering if he would ever come again.

"Maybe…" he thought, "…especially if there's pizza. But, *no one here is like me.*"

After the club, Camryn spoke with Andy. Andy mentioned to Camryn that Jason wasn't acting like himself. He was quiet at the club. They both recalled Jason slipping two more slices of the pizza into his backpack when no one was looking. It wasn't unlike him to do that, but usually he didn't do it in secret. They wondered if Jason would ever come back. Andy wondered if he could be the kind of friend who would be able to share Jesus with Jason.

* * *

Poverty is lacking the material resources needed for survival. Not having those resources can lead to despair, hopelessness and personal anguish. This lack also presents serious health problems that could potentially lead to death. In the United States most people have what they need to survive, though not all live at an equal level of privilege.

Much like a life of poverty, an underprivileged life can lead to a similar feeling of despair and a lack of hope.

But these symptoms are also a sign of a greater disease, completely rooted in sin. Sin is *spiritual poverty*. We can give people some relief from symptoms, but without Jesus, they are without the cure.

Love Fully—In Words and Actions

In finding Jesus we have found what everyone needs. With God's Spirit at work, we will find ourselves in situations where we can share Jesus and become, as one evangelist said, "a beggar telling another beggar where he found bread." Jesus called himself "the bread of life." He said, "whoever comes to me will never go hungry..."[1]

But we should not look past people's physical need to care for their spiritual need. God sees the underprivileged and their physical needs. Psalm 9:18 says, "But God will never forget the needy; the hope of the afflicted will never perish."[2] Scripture also states that God is looking out for the underprivileged, "You rescue the poor from those too strong for them, the poor and needy from those who rob them."[3] And also in Scripture we find that showing honor to others will help them see the glory of God.[4] Truly, God cares for the justice, dignity and well being of the underprivileged, and so should we. Sharing physical *and* spiritual bread is the right and honorable thing to do. So, give physical and spiritual care.

Love Blindly—Be a True Friend

God's love for us isn't affected by the level of our bank account, or by how big our house is. Our love for those around us should be just as blind. If you avoid being friends with people because they don't wear nice clothes, because they are on the school lunch program, because they live in a small house, or for some other superficial reason, the first thing you need to do is repent—now! God *despises* your rotten attitude towards the underprivileged.[5] Adjust your attitude by being thankful for the undeserved gift God gave you at the cross. Ask God's forgiveness, then decide to make a change in your actions.

Make this commitment: regardless of anyone's level of privilege, you will love them like God does: blindly. Start by just being a true friend. Friends talk to each other and have meaningful conversations, so make that your goal. Get to know the underprivileged around you in meaningful and sincere ways. Do not do it to rid yourself of a guilty conscience, do it because you want to have a new long-term friend and you want to connect that friend to Jesus.

Love Equally

Loving equally means creating a friendship that is equal in value, time, and energy to most of your other friendships. If it's anything less than that, then you've created something other than a true friendship. Friendship doesn't just mean conversation, it means hanging out together. But that can also create a problem, because hanging out usually requires money. An underprivileged friend may never offer to cover you for a movie, or to join their family for a trip to a theme park. They are not being thoughtless. Their day-to-day life may not include money for a movie, or going to a concert. When there is money involved, if your friend is struggling, offer to cover them because you're friends—not because they don't have any money.

Love with Dignity

Sometimes being underprivileged can feel so hopeless that it seems like it's impossible to survive without help from everyone around. It feels like handouts are necessary just to live. When a person is dependent on everyone else in order to survive, it can feel like there is no dignity left in life, because he or she cannot provide the basics for living. Don't let your friendship become like this. Continually offering your resources is not the best plan. So love with dignity. In the long-run, loving with dignity may mean planning your hang out times around activities and events that cost little or nothing, or just having friends over to your house. That costs nothing at all. And doing so will give them a greater chance to provide to you what they *can* offer—friendship.

Invite to Community

When your friendship begins to develop, be sure to invite your new friend to youth group and to church. The more Christian friends, love and support you can surround people with, the more likely they are to become committed to Jesus and stay committed in the long run. That's because we all need a community. When it comes to the church, money should have nothing to do with community! That kind of thinking doesn't belong in the Body of Christ. Bring them to youth events, and have a word with your youth pastor about potential scholarship opportunities for the big events.

Having a Conversation

• **What's one of the best things that has ever happened to you?** Learn about their life, their story, see the world though their eyes. Be prepared to share one of the best things that has happened to you—connect your story to Jesus.

•   **What's one of the toughest things that has ever happened to you?** Take time to listen to their sufferings. You are caring for your friend as you listen to them. If you have the opportunity to share one of your toughest times, be sure to include how God or the church or your youth group helped you through it.

•   **Do you wanna hang out at my house this weekend? What would you do this weekend if you could do anything?** Invite them into your life and hang out together. Jesus did this with his disciples. The second question is aimed at valuing them. What could you do together that shows you care about what they value? Doing this can make a lasting impact in their life.

•   **Jesus described himself as having nowhere to live, as homeless (Matthew 8:20). What does it mean when the most famous person in human history talks this way? Who do you believe Jesus was?** You have an opportunity to understand how they see poverty and Jesus. You will also have the opportunity to share who you believe Jesus to be.

---

[1] John 6:35 NIV.
[2] NIV.
[3] Psalm 35:10b NIV.
[4] 1 Peter 2:12.
[5] Psalm 18:27, Proverbs 14:31, 1 John 3:17.

GOD
SO
LOVED....

18

MY PARENTS

Tristan Jepson

"You just think you're better than we are!" My father's angry words snapped and hung in the air—all but leaving me speechless. Not only did I not know how to respond in that moment, it was also a difficult heart-check moment for me. It wasn't true...was it? Even if it wasn't my intention, evidently my actions and attitude were sending an unintended message.

I had grown up and still lived in a home where drugs and anger were the norm. I was eleven years-old when I was first offered drugs; it was at a party my father brought me to and I managed to say "no." My sister and I fearfully avoided our father most of the time because we could never tell whether the drugs he took made him more or less angry. We were never sure what kind of situation we'd be walking into when he was around. Our mother, who tried to avoid his anger as much as we did, attempted to console us. She would say, "That's just how he is," and, "You know he loves you; he just doesn't know how to show it."

School was an escape from my home life and I was usually very happy to be there. I was probably the only kid who hated snow days because I just wanted to be out of the house. I was also extremely skilled at acting like everything was fine all the time. Even my closest friends had no idea what my home life was like. I was an expert at covering up and ignoring any pain or brokenness. Good grades were a way to earn approval and I quickly found myself deeply rooted in a habit of people-pleasing to try to earn approval, acceptance, and maybe even love.

I was a Freshman in High School when a friend from leadership class invited me to something called "youth group." Regardless of the fact that I had to ask what it was and had never set foot inside a church before, I immediately said yes. The next week I went to youth group and encountered a God who knew my brokenness and loved me anyway.

When I met Jesus things began to change inside me and I started on a journey of transformation, but I still went home each night to the same problems and pain. Truthfully, it wasn't that I wanted to be better than my family as much as I felt I was being called to be different than who I used to be. Not only was the process of allowing God to change me difficult, it was also vastly imperfect.

There was virtually no one who saw me and my many flaws as clearly as my family did. I would hear, "You just think you're better than us," when I tried to change. If I didn't change, I would hear, "I thought you called yourself a Christian." I didn't know how to please them, much less reach them with the hope of the Gospel.

Learning to please God and not man while also learning to honor your parents and attempting to show who Jesus is through your life can feel like an impossible balancing act. Although the people closest to you might have a front row seat to your mistakes, they also have the best vantage to see Jesus do something incredible.

I had to learn that my parents weren't the enemy, even though it sometimes felt like they were. I had to learn to do my best to walk and live humbly and show them honor, regardless of whether I felt they deserved it, even when I felt I was right and they were wrong. Being "right" isn't a fruit of the Spirit and I couldn't hold my parents accountable to standards that they didn't even hold themselves to. I also had to start praying for them, but also for God to do a work in my heart. I needed God to heal my bitterness, hurt, and resentment so that I could begin to see them the way He did.

My parents and sister were hurting and broken just as much as I was—probably more than I could have known. While this didn't excuse or justify the things that went on in our home, realizing this helped me to see my family differently. I no longer saw them simply through a lens of hurt, but I began to see them with compassion. The same God who saw me and had started a good work in me also saw them and loved them.

If you're following Jesus while living in a home that doesn't, your parents are part of your mission field. If this feels overwhelming, complicated, or just plain impossible - you're in good company. I also felt that way. What seems like an obstacle can actually be an opportunity. We serve a God who wants to use the things Satan plans for destruction for our good—rough family relationships included. God redeems and restores.

Luke 8 contains a great story about a man who had an encounter with Jesus and was then sent home to proclaim the good news to his family. Jesus and His disciples had just arrived in the region of the Gerasenes, across the lake from Galilee. A demon-possessed man ran up to Jesus as soon as He got out of the boat. He was naked and had been living in a tomb, he'd been cutting himself, and he was able to break free from anything that was used to restrain him. He was essentially the crazy guy in town.

After a brief conversation, Jesus delivered the man completely and sent the demons that were possessing the man into a nearby herd of pigs (Luke 8:33). The townspeople saw the man sitting clothed and in his right mind. They were so shocked and afraid at everything that had happened that they asked Jesus to leave. The man who had been delivered begged to go with Jesus, but Jesus sent him back to his family to tell them everything God had done for him.

That is exactly what he did; he began to tell the entire town what Jesus had done. How awkward must that have been? Everyone would have known this guy's business. They would have seen him at the lowest point in his life. They would've known his past and his shame. Jesus knew all of this and sent the man anyway.

Let God Send You Home

Jesus sent the man home to proclaim the good news despite the difficulty involved. In fact, because Jesus was no longer welcome in Gerasenes, this man became the one person who could tell his family and neighbors about Jesus. It probably wasn't easy for the man, but he did it. It's the same with us. We get to be the ones to proclaim Jesus and the miracles He's done to our families. It might not be easy, but it's very important. You are the one who has access to your parents. You are the one that God is sending to bring the good news of Jesus. God sees you and the family you are in. You are not alone. Pray for your parents. Pray that God would help you to start to see them in the same way He does.[1]

Let God Transform You

Romans 12:2 says that we should let God transform us into a new person—even the way we think should be changed by God. The demon-possessed man changed after encountering Jesus, and we should change too. You will get opportunities to talk about how Jesus impacts your life, but your parents will also begin to see the change in you. This will happen when you throw off the sin that so easily tangles you up and embrace your life as a new creation. Talk to Jesus and wrestle with what it means to honor your parents; ask God to show you what that looks like. Seek the empowerment and filling of the Holy Spirit and allow Him to produce fruit of the Spirit in your life (see Galatians 5:22-23).

Your family won't be able to see what Jesus is doing in your life if you're not around, so make the most of the time you have with them. It can be easy to start to feel like you have more in common with your church community, but don't forget that God wants to reveal Himself to your parents through you. Think of things you can do to serve your parents that authentically shows the love of Jesus.

Don't Be Discouraged

When conflict or discouraging things happen, remind yourself that the weight of the burden doesn't lie on you. You aren't responsible for changing anyone, but you do get the opportunity and responsibility of proclaiming Jesus with both your words and with your life in a way that sows seeds of hope. In the same way that actual seeds can take a while to grow, seeds of hope can take a while to grow in your parents. There are always unseen things happening under the surface; God is at work even when we don't see it.

If you mess up and your parents give you a hard time, or if they bring up something from the past, try not to be discouraged. Instead, humble yourself. If you've messed up, apologize and ask for forgiveness. Refuse to carry bitterness towards them. Remember—although you might feel like you're in a battle, your parents are not the enemy. Ask God constantly to work in and through you, and be encouraged that God is the leading expert in using imperfect people to accomplish His extraordinary purposes.

Having a Conversation

Trying to see your parents the way Jesus does means humbly recognizing that there are some things we don't know. Look for opportunities to ask questions that might deepen your relationship with

126

them and also allow you an opportunity to share Jesus. Here are some questions you can try.

- **How was your day? How can I help?** This might sound overly simplistic, but ask it with no strings attached and no motives other than to show love to your parents. Listen and really hear them. As you listen, you might start to see ways you can serve them or help make their lives easier. Then help them! Anything you can do that is selfless (not about you) and serves them will probably get their attention.

- **Have I said "thank you" lately?** Speaking of getting your parents attention, try gratitude. Depending on your specific relationship with your parent(s) this might be tough, but gratitude shows that you honor them and what they've done for you. Gratitude is good for our relationships and our souls. If you have primarily had a negative outlook towards your family, invite God to start changing it through gratitude.

- **What was your experience with _____ like?** Fill in the blank with anything they've done recently or that you'd like to know more about. Showing that you value your parents' experience or opinions enough to ask is another way to show honor and deepen your understanding of them. You don't have to agree with them in order to hear them out, and you're showing that you're open to deeper conversations. Eventually you might get to topics of spiritual significance and might get an open door to share your perspective and experience.

- **Would you be willing to come to church with me?** Give your parent(s) opportunities to say yes without nagging or guilting them. Even if they don't say "yes" the first (or second, or third) time you invite them, let them know they are wanted. This is another heart check moment, because sometimes we might start to feel like church is "our thing" or feel awkward or vulnerable expressing our faith while they're "watching". Fight through these obstacles and keep proclaiming what Jesus has done.

---

[1] This doesn't mean you should silently stay in an abusive household. Asking for help from a trusted adult and getting out of that situation is important.

GOD
SO
LOVED....

<u>19</u>

SIBLINGS

Rob Gillen

"Where you going?" my sister asked as she sat at our kitchen table brushing her hair.

"I'm going to youth group." I grabbed a can of soda from the fridge and forced my foot into a worn-out sneaker.

She furrowed her brow. "What's youth group?"

I slipped on a jacket that smelled of cigarette smoke. "It's like church, but it's a bunch of teenagers. And there's food and games and stuff." A car horn beeped outside. I stood to my feet. "You should come some time. I'm not sure if you're old enough though. I'll ask PJ."

Rebecca stood up. I brushed past her. "What do you mean? Who's PJ?"

"Mom! Tony's here!" I yelled into the living room.

"Be safe! And give Tony some gas money!" my mom yelled back.

"PJ is the youth pastor," I said to Rebecca. "He's the guy in charge."

"...and don't get in a car with any strangers!" my mom finished. Rebecca and I smirked at each other and shook our heads.

"Mom, I'm a sixteen-year-old-guy! Seriously?!"
"You heard me!" she insisted.

I grabbed a handful of coins from our change can and forced on my second sneaker. The coins were greasy from the oil on my dad's hands. He'd found most of them on school buses he'd repaired. The car horn beeped again.

My dad walked in wearing his dark blue coveralls and grabbed a beer from the fridge. "When you gettin' home?" he asked in a deep voice.

"We're hanging out after youth group, but Tony's giving me a ride back."

"You better go." He sat down to take off his boots. "I told Tony if you keep him waiting he should charge you double!" he joked cheesily. "You have enough money?"

"Yeah, I'm good. Thanks!"

"Love you."

"Love you too!" I yelled from outside as the screen door slammed shut behind me.

My sister watched through a small kitchen window as I jumped into Tony's old silver Ford Probe. The bass from his Christian metal music shook the windows as we backed out of my parent's driveway and sped away.

I can't imagine what was going through my sister's head those first few weeks. Our parents had only taken us to church a couple of times as young children, usually while visiting a distant family member. Both her and I were completely in the dark when it came to things of God, church, or anything religious. That all changed when my girlfriend was invited to youth group, and I reluctantly joined her. Our relationship didn't last, but my relationship with Christ stuck like glue.

In a matter of weeks I was fully committed. I was attending anything and everything the church was doing, and I was talking about it—a lot! I remember how everyday felt like a new adventure. It was the most exhilarating time of my life! But my sister was on the outside looking in. All she knew was that I seemed a lot happier and I looked like I had a plan all of sudden—a purpose for living. It was as if I knew everything was going to be ok.

She wouldn't be on the outside for very long though. Soon Rebecca would discover that some of her friends in school attended the same youth group I did. In a matter of months she was attending and she too had given her life to Jesus.

God adores your siblings—bad habits, personality quirks and all! He loves your siblings more than you love them, and He wants them to know Him more than you do, and more than they know!

It's truly impossible to understand just how much He loves us. The Bible tells us that *"God demonstrates his own love for us in this: While we were still sinners, Christ died for us."*[1] This verse has to be the perfect example of just *how little* our relationship with God is about us, and just *how much* it's about Him and His perfect love. Jesus gave His life on the cross for your sibling just as much as He did for you. He longs to have you both! He dreamed your sibling into existence.

One of the ways God loves your sibling is *through you.* 1 John 4:21 reads, "He has given us this command: Anyone who loves God must also love their brother and sister."[2] Jesus was talking about relationships in the church, but he was using family terms to describe those relationships. He is commanding that we love our "brother" (or the men in our lives) and our "sister" (the women in our lives). God is using sibling relationships as an example for the kind of relationships we should have in the church. If that's how we should treat our brothers and sisters in the church, how much more should we embrace our biological siblings with the love of God?

As an individual who knows Jesus, you are Christ's ambassador to your home. By default and by design, you naturally inherit the calling to reach your family. It's not a burden; it's a *privilege!* God's desire to use you to reach your family is something to cherish. We don't *have to* be light in the darkness, we *get to* be light. We *get to* be Jesus' voice to our family. It is the highest honor.

Pray for your Sibling

Francis Chan wrote, *"Prayer is a way of walking in love."*[3] When we love someone in need (especially those with the greatest need – salvation), we pray for him or her. Pray consistently and full-of-faith that your loved ones will come to know Jesus. Then, release them to God. He has a great plan for your sibling.

I had a great youth pastor who taught me to pray for my family. I knew that God had an awesome plan for Rebecca, just like He had an awesome plan for me. Right from the start, I began praying for her. At night, I would include her in a list of prayer needs. I would pray for her sometimes as we were getting ready for school in the morning and when

I was at the altar at youth group. I would pray for her at youth retreats and I would pray for her during our high school's campus bible club. Praying for your sibling is as simple as agreeing with the desire and the vision that God already has for them.

Live It Out

For the majority of people you try to share Jesus with, there will only be a few opportunities for an in-person encounter—not so with your siblings. If you're living a life devoted to Christ, they're going to see it. But don't just go through the motions, live it out with passion!

As Mark Batterson puts it, *"Go all-in and all-out for the All-in-All!"*[4] Don't hold back! I never had to tell my sister I was excited about God; she knew it because of how I lived my life. I was clearing my schedule for church-related activities. I was rearranging my relationships. I was tithing my money in the offering and giving sacrificially to missions. I was taking my Bible to school and reading it at our kitchen table. It was obvious to anyone close to me that I wasn't playing around. This was real, and I was living it out.

Be Humble

It's important to understand that if your sibling isn't following God and you are, it could become confrontational at first. As their sibling, you could face some challenges with overcoming sibling stigmas, such as rivalries, jealousy and natural comparisons. Some examples of comments that reveal this would be: *"What makes you so special?"* or, *"All of a sudden you're so spiritual! You're no better than anyone in this family!"*

These responses are normal, especially if your sibling feels that you're getting special treatment from your parents because of your new lifestyle. Don't take offense to this. Instead, always admit your own faults. Emphasize that being a Christian doesn't mean that you're perfect or better than anyone else—it simply means you've been forgiven, discovered the truth, and you want others to experience it as well.

Having a Conversation

You probably know your sibling very well. Some of the questions below have been left with a blank. You can complete those questions and lead to a powerful conversation.

- **What's something interesting happening at** _____? (Insert their favorite hobby or sport). Take an interest in what's happening in your sibling's life. Your sibling will take an interest in you, in return. This is a great way to talk casually about Jesus and church!

- **What's one of your favorite memories from growing up together?** Be ready to answer this question after your sibling does. This is a great question for connecting and bonding.

- **What's the most important thing in life?** Listen carefully, and you'll learn the spiritual condition or priorities of your sibling. Be ready to share the most important thing in your life, which is Jesus.

- **Jesus had siblings too...what do you think it was like to be a sibling to Jesus?** If your sibling knows you're a Christ follower, this will not be an awkward question. It's just a great way to start talking about Jesus with your sibling.

- **Share 1 John 4:21 with your sibling. Why was this important to Jesus? What does that say about God and how we treat others?** This is a great way to open up a conversation about Jesus, and about God's love for us and the love we're to have for others. Be ready to share!

---

[1] Romans 5:8 NIV.

[2] NIV.

[3] Francis Chan, *Desiring God*, "Prayer As A Way of Walking In Love," (Desiring God Foundation: 2011), accessed January 11, 2016, http://www.desiringgod.org/messages/prayer-as-a-way-of-walking-in-love-a-personal-journey.

[4] Mark Batterson, *All In: You Are One Decision Away From A Totally Different Life* (Grand Rapids: Zondervan, 2013),14.

GOD
SO
LOVED....

<u>20</u>

THE ANGRY AND FRUSTRATED

Forrest Rowell

I was driving into town with my family one morning when we came to a red light. As we were sitting there, I noticed the car in front of us had a large sticker in the back window. It was impossible to ignore. It depicted a stick figure holding a gun to his head. It also had a statement on it, indicating the driver of the car, or whoever put the bumper sticker on it, hated his life.

It wasn't long before this sticker caught the attention of my whole family. Looking in the rearview mirror, I noticed a confused expression on the faces of my boys, who were seven and eight at the time.

"Dad, why is that guy holding a gun to his head?" my oldest son Rocco asked.

Before I could answer, Bruno chimed in, "Dad, what does that mean?"

An awkward, but necessary conversation followed. I explained to my boys that some people feel overwhelmed by life situations and circumstances, which can reach the point of throwing in the towel and taking their own lives. This was a thought that had never crossed my boys' minds before. They were living life the way kids their age should— happy, carefree, and unaffected by the broken world they will someday find themselves in. That day, as we sat at that intersection in our family van, they received a harsh taste of reality.

Our discussion ended a few minutes later, but it stuck with me for much longer.

I let this stir in my mind and heart for a while, until I began to see pain in a new light. It's something we all go through in our lives. The question is not if we will experience pain, but when. Pain affects us all in different ways. Something that gets one person down for a few weeks can keep another person down for a lifetime. The way that we deal with our pain is crucial; it has more of an impact on our lives than the pain itself. Pain can drive a person to become very angry and frustrated if it's not dealt with appropriately.

A few years ago, I walked into a church in my city, but I wasn't there for church. Dressed in a dark colored suit, the mood was sober as hundreds of people filled the sanctuary. There are always more tears at the funeral of a teenager. Tension filled the room; you could sense the pain, the unanswered questions. It's hard enough to attend the funeral of someone who lived life to the full, but nearly unbearable to attend the funeral of someone who had a blank slate before them. There were plenty of visibly shaken students painting a picture of what it was to be angry or frustrated.

At the reception, I got a plate of food and sat down at an open table. It wasn't long before a student named Mike joined me. He was visibly upset, much like the rest, but not just because his friend and classmate had been shot and killed. As we began to talk he told me that he was upset at the situation and circumstance, but also by the conversations taking place around him.

I asked what he meant by this, and he told me that while he was waiting in line for his food he overheard several students who were set on revenge; they wanted to return evil for evil. Others were planning to go out that night and get trashed with drugs and alcohol in honor of the "Homie" they just lost. They wanted to space out and forget about life—forget about the pain—for as long as they could. Perhaps if they ran far enough from it they wouldn't have to feel it. They wouldn't have to ask themselves where their own lives were headed.

These students were angry, frustrated, and they didn't know how to handle it. Mike didn't want to go down this path; it was his senior year, and he wanted to make his life count. He wanted to finish high school strong and enter adulthood on the right path. He didn't want this tragedy to pull him away from his goals and dreams. He needed a voice urging him in the right direction. I encouraged him to stand up and be bold at his school over the next year. "Don't let this pain drag you down," I told him. "Let it be the very thing that pushes you forward."

Emotional pain has the potential to leave far bigger scars on our lives than physical pain ever could. One of my first big encounters with emotional pain was as a freshman in high school. It was my first dance and I had a date—life couldn't get much better! After a nice dinner, we headed to the dance. I thought everything was going great, but it wasn't long before I was officially *ditched*. It's hard to describe how terrible this experience made me feel, but this is one of the worst ways you can be rejected.

Then there was the moment when my parents decided it would be best to part ways—they were getting divorced. That brought a lot of emotional mess into my life. As a matter of fact it really left me feeling as though I was at a breaking point. Everything inside of me wanted to go out and make some really stupid decisions, but God brought some great friends and leaders into my life that helped me process my life and where I was headed.

If you have a friend who is angry and frustrated, there's a very good chance that a severe emotional pain lies deep under the surface of their actions. Ultimately, a life fully submitted to Christ is well equipped to deal with the emotional pain life throws at it. However, before you can share Jesus with a frustrated or angry student, you probably need to take the time to help them through the challenges they are facing.

Be a Voice of Peace

When I met with Mike at the funeral, he was hearing a lot of voices urging him to move in a lot of angry and frustrated directions. He needed to hear a voice of peace, a voice of reason. You can help your angry or frustrated friend by being that voice of peace. The Holy Spirit helps us with this. Philippians 4:7 says, "And the peace of God, which surpasses all understanding, will guard your hearts and your minds in Christ Jesus."[1]

In the face of their anger or frustration, don't respond with an equal amount of emotional energy. Instead, remain calm and listen to what they have to say. When they're ready for you to say something, let them know you're here for them, you care for them, and you don't want them to do anything drastic. Encourage them! Let them know life will not always be this way, and there is a better way to approach these challenges than doing something they may regret.

Speak Truth in Love[2]

This student generation must be reminded about what the Bible says about them. If most of what they hear about themselves are negative messages, they aren't hearing the full truth. Here's what Psalm 139 says about each individual:

> Oh yes, you shaped me first inside, then out;
>   you formed me in my mother's womb.
> I thank you, High God—you're breathtaking!
> Body and soul, I am marvelously made![3]

Your angry or frustrated friend needs to know—he is a unique, one-of-a-kind masterpiece that God created! There never has been and never will be another one of him on the planet! Speak this truth from your heart—let them know they matter to you and they matter to God.

Provide a Place of Refuge

A place of refuge is a shelter where someone is protected and kept safe from danger or trouble. One of the most practical things you can do to share the love of God with an angry or frustrated student is to provide them an escape by inviting them into a loving and affirming environment. This might be your home, where loving Christian parents can encourage them, in addition to your own encouragement. The place of refuge could also be your church for youth group, where they will be welcomed with open arms, and finding caring adults who will listen and encourage. Don't leave an angry or frustrated student where they are, and don't encourage them with your words only. Demonstrate that you are sincere by inviting them into these warm and welcoming environments.

Having a Conversation

An angry or frustrated student can often be defused, or redirected, with a listening ear and a great conversation. Here are some questions to get you going:

- **What's going on? Tell me about it.** If they seem angry or frustrated at the moment, this is a great question to ask. Start by listening. Don't tell them what to do or how to do it—just hear them out. Let them know you're there for them.

- **What was one of toughest moments that you've experienced in your life? How did you deal with that pain?** Not only will you hear a little bit about some of their life experience, you'll also find out how they deal with pain. Listen authentically, because when you do, you communicate that you care about their story. You'll probably have the opportunity to talk about your toughest moment. How did you deal with it? Is this a good time to talk about Jesus?

- Share Psalm 139, then ask, **"Did you know that you're God's creation? How does that make you feel?"** Be ready, because they may not answer like you think. If they don't believe in God, they may respond indifferently. If they do believe in God, they may be angry at how their life is going. Gently affirm your friend, let them know you hear them. But also reaffirm the Scriptures. Encourage them that they are fearfully and wonderfully made, whether they believe it or not.

- **I believe that pain can drive a person to become better or bitter in life, what do you think? What has your experience been?** Here's a great conversation to talk about dealing with the emotional pain we encounter in life. Ultimately, avoiding bitterness involves being able to forgive the past and the people who have hurt you. When we refuse to forgive the past, we carry the weight of the pain with us continually.

- **Do you think Jesus had a right to be angry or frustrated? What made it possible for Him to forgive us instead of becoming bitter?** Jesus suffered the ultimate injustice—dying for sins he did not commit to pay a debt He did not owe. Not only that, but He forgives us. Love is the key. This is a great opportunity to share the Gospel message.

---

[1] NIV.

[2] Ephesians 4:15.

[3] Verses 13-14, The Message.

GOD
SO
LOVED....

21
THE BULLIED

Rob Gillen

Agnes walked into the cold, empty classroom and sat her overloaded backpack down on the desk. Her thin, lanky frame almost tipped over as she swung the bag off her shoulder. She quickly slid into her desk and pulled out some notes from yesterday. She was the first in homeroom today, just like every other day. Her mom drops her off early, trying to make it to work on time.

A group of girls entered the room laughing and talking loudly. Agnes sat up straight and started fixing her unkempt, red hair, repeatedly glancing over at the girls out of the corner of her eye.

The girls sat down next to one another on the opposite side of the room.

Agnes started scribbling on her notebook, trying to look busy.

The room grew quiet.

"I feel so bad for her," one girl whispered.

Agnes flinched.

"What year is she?" another asked.

Some other students walked into the room, along with the teacher.

"I think she's an exchange student," one girl shrugged. "But I'm pretty sure I've seen her wear those pants four times this week."

They laughed under their breath.

A boy sat down beside the girls. "Who you talking about?" He asked not-so-quietly.

"Miss America over there." She gestured with a side-nod.

Agnes twisted her bony frame, trying to angle her back towards the group. She hunched over her notebook, scribbling frantically on the paper.

"You girls are relentless," the boy said smirking. "How many times is it this week? Cut her some slack, she's a freshmen."

Agnes perked up a little. She started picking at the edge of her notebook.

"Besides," he continued, "Even homeless people need a break."

The group broke out in laughter.

Others leaned in to find out what was so funny.

Agnes sat up straight and raised her hand.

"Uh oh," the boy whispered. "Ya'll are in trouble now."

More snickering. More laughter.

Agnes desperately asked, "Mrs. Edwards?"

The teacher jerked her head up. "Oh. Yes. What is it Aggie?"

The eyes of the room zeroed in on her.

"May I use the bathroom?" She jumped to her feet and began speed walking towards the door.

"Sure, but you'll need a pass."

Agnes kept moving with her head down and her arms straight down to her sides.

"Agnes? Agnes, you need a pass!"

She plowed through the door and made a beeline down the hallway. The teacher jumped up from her desk and made her way to the door. But Agnes had already made it to the bathroom. She ran to the first stall and locked the door behind her.

Have you met Agnes? You probably have. Most of us have met her at some point in our lives. Or maybe you were Agnes? When someone sticks out from the pack, they quickly become a target. Nearly a fourth of all students report being bullied; usually for their looks, body shape, or race.[1]

Bullying comes in a lot of different forms. Whether it's teasing, name-calling, taunting or being threatened, bullying can have a profound effect on the self-image of a student. Most effects of bullying aren't physical, but mental and emotional. The social aspects of bullying can be consistent and unrelenting. As we see with Agnes, they can follow you; sometimes for the rest of your life.

God has a special place in his heart for the vulnerable and the hurting. Psalms 46:1 tells us that, "God is our refuge and strength, an ever-present help in trouble."[2] We also read that He "is close to the brokenhearted and saves those who are crushed in spirit."[3]

2 Corinthians 1:3-4 says, "Blessed be God, the Father of our Lord Jesus Christ, the Father of mercies, and the God of all comfort, who comforts us in all our tribulation, that we may be able to comfort those who are in any trouble by the comfort with which we ourselves are comforted by God."[4] God genuinely cares about our hurts and our suffering; He loves the bullied!

Conversely, God absolutely despises bullying. Proverbs 6:16-19 says, "There are six things the LORD hates, seven that are detestable to him: haughty eyes, a lying tongue, hands that shed innocent blood, a heart that devises wicked schemes, feet that are quick to rush into evil, a false witness who pours out lies and a person who stirs up conflict in the community."[5] Notice that I did not say that God hates bullies, but that he despises their behavior. Believe it or not, God loves bullies. He hates bullying and what it's done to them and others, but He loves bullies.

Pray for the Bullied

Matthew 14:14 tells how Jesus was moved with compassion when He saw the needs of those around Him. In response to this compassion that moved Him, Jesus began to minister healing to those around Him. Jesus is not only our healer; he is our role-model. Matthew said that Jesus *was moved*. The suffering that he saw gripped his heart. We should be moved with compassion when we see the bullied as well. Pray that God will fill you with compassion for the hurting, so that you will be moved to do something about it.

Be Kind and Affirming

Being bullied is a very painful experience, and has proven to be much more damaging than most understand. If the target student is in the midst of being bullied, or has just been bullied recently, they may feel very bad about themselves and are probably experiencing a lot of dark feelings about themselves and about life in general.[6]

It's important that you are highly sensitive to be encouraging and uplifting to a student who has been bullied. Find simple ways to compliment them, and always be looking for ways to affirm them. Find common ground with them. What do you two have in common? Point it out! This will help them see that they're not abnormal or alone. Everyone experiences challenges—that's just part of life.

Be a Source of Hope

When reaching out to the bullied, be careful not to give them a label, or treat them like a victim. Instead, treat them like a friend, or like anyone else you would meet for the first time. If the bullying incident is the start of your friendship, be sure to offer him or her hope that everything's going to work out, and that it won't last forever. Be a source of hope to them by letting them know they're a great person and that this will soon pass. Point out the positive things about your friend, the things you appreciate about them.

Help them find hope in an uplifting environment outside of school. Invite them into your home, or hangout together at another friend's house, and spend some quality friend time together beyond the bullying environment. Bring them with you to church or your youth group. Pay for them to attend the next youth retreat or event. Let them have a positive and uplifting experience with the Body of Christ, and they will find healing for their hurts.

Understand Your Limitations

It's important to understand that you are not a trained psychologist. Students who are bullied are far more likely to deal with depression and experience suicidal thoughts. If they are depressed, the best advice to give your friend is to seek help from your school's guidance counselor, or to speak with a trusted adult who can help them.

If your friend expresses a desire to commit suicide, you must help them get help from a trusted and responsible adult. Offer to go with them to a parent, guidance counselor, or pastor. If they refuse, or if the conversation becomes urgent, you must go to an adult that you trust on your friend's behalf. They may feel betrayed initially that you broke confidence, but in the end, they should realize that you only told someone because you were fearful for their safety, and their long-term health – that's what a *true friend* does!

Having a Conversation

A student who is bullied can use a great friend. Friendships begin with conversations. Some of the questions below can help you spark a powerful conversation:

- **What's a favorite hobby that you have? What makes it your favorite?** Take an interest in what's happening in your friend's life (apart from the bullying). This serves as a great way to get his/her mind off of the bullying, and once they are comfortable, they may eventually ask questions about your hobbies and interests.

- **What are you looking forward to this year? Tell me about it.** This is a great question because it focuses on the future – which is very bright! Be ready to share your response!

- **What's the most important thing in your life?** Listen carefully, and you'll learn the spiritual condition or priorities of your friend. Be ready to share the most important thing in your life, which is Jesus.

- **Jesus was abused and made fun of...why would God let His Son experience physical and emotional harm?** If your friend doesn't know you're a Christian, this will be a strong turning point in the conversation. Don't be afraid to go with it though, this will naturally explain why you're so kind and caring.

- **Share 2 Corinthians 1:3-4 with your friend. What do you think this verse says about God? What does it say about you and I and how he views us?** This is a great way to open up a conversation about Jesus, and a great way to discuss God's love. Be ready to share!

---

[1] National Bullying Prevention Center, "Bullying Statistics," accessed January 16, 2016, http://www.pacer.org/bullying/about/media-kit/stats.asp.

[2] NIV.

[3] Psalm 34:18-19 NIV.

[4] NIV.

[5] NIV.

[6] U.S. Department of Health and Human Services, "Facts About Bullying," accessed January 16, 2016, http://www.stopbullying.gov/news/media/facts/.

GOD
SO
LOVED....

22
THE CUTTER
Dave Freeland

Rachel seemed like a normal student, and she came from a loving family, but the pressure began to build in her life when she was 13 years old. Rachel's family began to fall apart shortly after the death of her grandfather. She felt it was her responsibility to hold the family together. In the midst of this tragedy, she went through a big break-up that pushed her over the edge. She was home alone, sobbing uncontrollably, and feeling like she couldn't handle life any longer. That was the first time she took a razor to her arm, cutting herself to escape the emotional pain of life.

That first experience led her into a downward spiral of mutilation. She believed the physical pain of cutting would relieve her of the emotional pain she was experiencing. Yet, as she continued to cut, she began to hate herself for reasons she couldn't explain. Rachel never thought cutting would become an addiction; she cut once every few days, but soon it became more frequent. Before long it became an out-of-control addiction that marked her entire body. She would cut each night before going to bed, any time she was alone, and every trip to the restroom.

The initial pain in the moment of cutting would only last a minute, but soon the emotional relief also disappeared. Cutting was no longer enough; Rachel's insecurities and selfishness led to anger. She tried to conceal the anger, but before long those close to her began to feel it. Her outbursts of anger took a toll on those she loved. Her anger led to deeper cuts, as she tried to damage herself more and more. Rachel felt there was no way out of the deep hole she dug herself into, and soon deep guilt began to set in.

We all handle the storms in our life differently, and many can relate to Rachel's story. There are many reasons why a person would harm herself. Rachel believed that her issue with cutting was due to her insecurity; how she felt about herself and her selfishness. In another sense, she wanted to punish herself for some reason that no one else, including her, understood.

Students that cut often feel hopeless; they believe they are all alone and no one cares. They are conflicted because they privately like the way cutting looks on their arms, but they are ashamed of what they've turned into and feel like they have to hide it. The longer they keep the scars hidden, the more they feel connected to the behavior. It's their secret, and they don't want to give it up. Because they believe no one cares, they also believe their behavior doesn't affect anyone, but it does. In fact, it affects everyone around them.

Cutting only masks the problems of life, and only for a short time; it doesn't make any problem go away. On the contrary, the emotional pain and torment only increase deep inside until it all spills out and affects everyone around. When Rachel's pain began to spill out in anger, her family began to notice. When they discovered the seriousness of her addiction, they got her professional help. It was at this time that Rachel met Jesus. She learned that God is our deliverer and our way out. Through a lot of discipline, anger, and tears, she found freedom from the bondage in her life—things that she carried for so long.

I asked Rachel, "What would you say to someone struggling with cutting?"

Her response was, "Let it go. It's not worth it. Talk with someone and get help." That first line of help—that first conversation a cutting student has with someone who can help—may come from someone like you who notices the pain and shows genuine care and interest. God so loved the cutter, and so should you.

While cutting students may feel hopeless, God's word is full of hope for them. Jeremiah 29:11 says, "'For I know the plans I have for you,' declares the Lord, 'plans to prosper you and not to harm you, plans to give you hope and a future.'"[1]

Rachel's favorite scripture is 1 Peter 2:21-25:

> To this you were called, because Christ suffered for you, leaving you an example, that you should follow in his steps. He committed no sin, and no deceit was found in his mouth. When they hurled their insults at him he did not retaliate; when he suffered, he made no threats. Instead, he entrusted himself to him who judges justly. He himself bore our sins in his body on the cross, so that we might die to sins and live for righteousness; by his wounds you have been healed. For you were like sheep going astray, but now you have returned to the Shepherd and overseer of our souls.[2]

God's Word has power and authority in our lives. Rachel said, "This passage helped me so much once I made the decision to give up my strongholds and give my life to Christ. It always reminds me that it is by His stripes, not mine, that I am healed. And that I no longer have to be a slave to that addiction because that price has already been paid for me and for that I am so thankful." Jesus decided to take all the pain on the cross! He was cut so others wouldn't have to be. It's through His stripes, not ours, that we find healing!

I knew a student named Grace; a devoted follower of Jesus who had committed herself as a missionary to her high school campus—a Campus Missionary. Grace began to pray as she walked from class to class for opportunities and direction from the Holy Spirit. One day she heard God speak, turned around, and walked up to a girl she didn't know. Grace said, "I know you don't know me, but I pray every day as I walk through these halls and God spoke to me about you. He wants you to know that He loves you and that you don't have to cut yourself anymore because He wore those stripes on the cross for you. He wants to take the hurt and pain that is in your life, and show you that He loves and understands, and that there is freedom for you."

Grace prayed for her and they both hurried off to their next class. Later that day the girl was looking for Grace and found her after school. She said, "I don't know how you know those things about me, but everything you said is true. I just wanted to say thank you for sharing with me today. I didn't know anyone cared, but now I know people do care and that God loves and cares for me."

Pray for Vision and Opportunities

There are countless numbers of students who walk the halls and carry the scars of life on their arms. They feel lost and hopeless, but usually hide the pain and the scars. Pray that God will give you vision to see this pain supernaturally, and provide you with guidance to begin a conversation. As you pray throughout the day on your school campus, God will lead you to opportunities. He will begin to reveal to you, through the Holy Spirit, who needs His love desperately.

Share God's Promises, the Gospel, and Your Life

The promises of hope in Scripture, like Jeremiah 29:11, may be the brightest rays of hope a cutting student has heard in a long time. Always be encouraging to students that cut, and assure them that God sees their pain. Genesis 16 tells the story of Hagar, a servant who had been abused and ran away. An angel of the Lord found Hagar and assured her, "the Lord has heard of your misery."[3] Hagar was amazed that anyone even knew of her pain. She gave God a special name that day, *El Roi*, when she said, "You are the God who sees me."[4] Just like the angel who found Hagar, you can assure hurting students that God sees them and cares about their pain.

The Gospel teaches us that Jesus suffered with cuts and wounds so that we could experience healing. Share the truth of the Gospel through 1 Peter 2:21-25, the passage of Scripture that made such a difference in Rachel's life. Ask if you can pray with your friend. Take things a step further by inviting her to be a part of your life. Establish a friendship, invest in her, let her into your life and invite her into your youth group. She needs long-term support, friendship, and discipleship.

Get Help

Cutting is not a harmless addiction; it can lead to serious mental and physical health issues, and even death when it is carried too far. When you realize someone is cutting, you must get help from a qualified adult for that person. Start by asking him or her to go with you to someone who can be trusted to help, such as a parent, a youth pastor,

pastor, or a guidance counselor or teacher. If a cutting student refuses to go with you to a qualified adult, you must report the problem to a teacher, guidance counselor, or pastor. That may seem difficult, but the consequences of cutting behavior are far too serious to ignore.

Having a Conversation

A cutting student needs a friend, and friendship begins with conversation. Here are some questions that can help you have powerful conversations:

- **How are things going in your life? Tell me about it.**

- **What are some of the biggest stresses in your life right now? What makes it so stressful?**

- **Will you pray with me? What can I pray with you for?**

- **Share 1 Peter 2:21-25. What does it mean when it says, "by his wounds you have been healed"?**

---

[1] NIV.
[2] The Message.
[3] Genesis 16:11 NIV.
[4] Genesis 16:13 NIV.

GOD
SO
LOVED....

23

LGBT STUDENTS

Wes Sheley

While youth pastoring in Klamath Falls, Oregon, I began to see a growing trend within our students in the community and our youth ministry. This growing trend was the emergence of same sex attraction and the LGBT lifestyle among teenagers. At one point we had 12-15 students that were gay or had thoughts of being gay. Most of the students didn't start off in our youth ministry, but began attending because they felt accepted. I watched as God developed our students' hearts to accept everyone who walked through the doors of our youth ministry, despite their beliefs or lifestyles. This was not an overnight process, but it was a journey. That journey all started when the one openly gay student in town came walking into our youth room.

It was a typical Wednesday night discipleship class. One of our students was a friend to this young man and invited him to come and join us. I wish you could have seen the faces of our students when he walked in—the looks were of shock and disbelief. I welcomed him and invited him in, but his friend wasn't there yet, so he stepped outside of the room to wait. When he stepped out, you could see and hear the whispers between the other students. I don't know what they were whispering, but I'm sure it was something like, "What is he doing here?" They weren't doing this to be mean—they were just amazed.

When his friend showed up and they entered the room, I witnessed what I would describe as God's love filling the air. Student after student welcomed this young man to our youth group and made him feel loved. We just began a series talking about worship and the history behind the songs we sing. This was one reason he came that night, because he was in the high school choir and was interested in the topic. He not only attended, but also participated in our discussions, and the other students

153

continued to interact with him. At the end of the night he said he would be back.

He showed up the following Tuesday for our regular youth night. He asked to speak to me, so we went into my office. He began to share, with tears in his eyes, that he visited most youth groups in town at one point or another, but never felt this accepted by any of them. He continued to tell me that he had a great time last Wednesday, and on the next day three of our high school students approached him at different times and apologized for the way they had treated him in the past.

I would like to say that this young man asked Jesus into his life that week, but that's not how it went. We planted the seed of the Gospel, and we started watering it. This young man continued to come to youth faithfully. He knew what we believed, and what the Word of God says about the LGBT lifestyle. We never focused on his sin; we focused on *our sins*, and most importantly, God's grace and love.

But Jesus went to the Mount of Olives. At dawn he appeared again in the temple courts, where all the people gathered around him, and he sat down to teach them. The teachers of the law and the Pharisees brought in a woman caught in adultery. They made her stand before the group and said to Jesus, "Teacher, this woman was caught in the act of adultery. In the Law Moses commanded us to stone such women. Now what do you say?" They were using this question as a trap, in order to have a basis for accusing him.

But Jesus bent down and started to write on the ground with his finger. When they kept on questioning him, he straightened up and said to them, "Let any one of you who is without sin be the first to throw a stone at her."

Again he stooped down and wrote on the ground.

At this, those who heard began to go away one at a time, the older one first, until only Jesus was left, with the woman still standing there.

Jesus straightened up and asked her, "Woman, where are they? Has no one condemned you?"

"No one, sir," she said.

*"Then neither do I condemn you," Jesus declared. "Go now and
leave your life of sin."*
John 8:1-11 NIV

John 8 shows us a deep difference between two ways of dealing
with sin. The first way is shown by a group of religious people, standing
in the place of judge and jury, ready to condemn and punish a woman
clearly caught violating God's commands in the Law. The accused
woman must have viewed this group as judgmental and full of hate. She
probably wished they would mind their own business. Does this sound
familiar? We see the same thing happening today in our culture, but with
different people and different accusations. Religious leaders accuse the
LGBT groups, and the LGBT groups view the religious as full of hate
for them because of their lifestyle.

The second way of dealing with sin is shown by Jesus. He hears
the accusations of the religious leaders, and He doesn't argue against
them. In fact, He knows they are *right* in their accusations, but He also
demonstrates why they are *wrong* in how they are dealing with the
situation. The religious leaders want to hand out the consequences of sin
themselves, and in doing so, want to establish some kind of false
superiority over the woman. But in reality, they have no superiority, and
neither do we. Jesus shows us the way of grace, because all but Him
have sinned, and none of us have the right to cast the first stone.

Listen

Jesus took time to listen to the story that was being shared. We
must also take the time to listen. We must find common ground with
those that we are reaching out to. Even though, in this passage, it was
not the woman sharing her story but her accusers, Jesus took time to
listen to her story. Everyone has a story behind what makes them who
they are, and that includes you. Listen patiently, and let your actions
speak for themselves.

Stand Up

We need to stand up for LGBT students. Let me clarify what I
mean. Jesus demonstrated this by defending the adulterous woman
without accepting her sin. He fought for the individual by showing
compassion and pointing out that we are in no place to judge, because
each of us has our own sin. We must stand up for the individual's soul
above all other things, while neither accepting nor endorsing sin. The
life of every student matters—it matters to God and it should matter to
us. God so loved the LGBT.

155

Be Faithful

One thing that stands out to me is that after everyone left this woman in her situation, Jesus was still there. We must be the ones that are faithful, because Jesus is always faithful. We must work twice as hard to build bridges between us and the LGBT groups than any other group on our school campuses. The only way we can do this is to be faithful in love and in action.

Secondly, be faithful with God's Word—honor it by being a Christian of integrity and humility. People are waiting for us to stumble and live up to the 'hypocrite' title the world loves to put on Christians. When you make a mistake, admit it. When you want to quit, don't. When your beliefs are tested, be strong. Jesus was able to love the adulterous woman and speak truth into her life and send her on her way. We must earn the right to do the same with the LGBT community. We must be faithful.

Having a Conversation

Here are some questions to help you have great conversations that could lead to Jesus. Some of these will help you have a personal conversation that leads to Jesus, while others will help you connect with some of the broader things God may be wanting to do in your school.

- **What are some of your favorite things to do? Tell me about that.** Just take the time to get to know them better. Take an interest in their interests. Having a great conversation with an LGBT student is pretty much like having a great conversation with anyone else. If they ask you, tell them what you love to do. I pray going to church, reading the Bible, serving others, and worship will be among them.

- **What is the most exciting thing you are looking forward to in the next few months?** Maybe it will be a holiday, vacation, or an accomplishment. Listen closely, because whatever they find exciting may also be an indication of what's important to them. Be prepared with your response, as well.

- **What are some of the greatest challenges you are facing in life?** This is a more serious question, and they may have some pretty serious things to share with you. Listen and listen closely. Follow up with more questions based upon what you hear. When the time is right, ask if you can pray with them about these challenges.

- **If you could ask God anything, what would you ask Him?**
  Your friend may not even believe God exists, but it's still an
  interesting question to consider. They may ask God a question
  that you think you know the answer to, but don't be too quick
  to answer on God's behalf. It's more important to listen. It's
  likely the question they would ask may also contain the deep
  feelings they'd like to express. When it's your turn, share your
  response.

GOD
SO
LOVED....

24

THE LONELY

James Marti

It was a Friday night like most others; I was walking home after a high school football game wondering why I felt so alone. I was quite involved in my high school. I played football, ran track, played the saxophone in the marching, concert, and jazz bands, and I was the winningest wrestler on the school's squad. I even went to the Christian club every week.

I grew up in a small town in central California where everybody knew one another, but for some reason every Friday night I walked home by myself, feeling the same way...alone. I began to blame God. It was His fault I was not with my friends drinking and hooking up with girls. I hated Mondays because everyone would spend the morning recounting the exploits of their weekend activities. After listening to their stories, I felt more alone and left out than ever. Was this the kind of life God wanted me to have? Why couldn't I do all the things my friends were having so much fun doing? I held back the tears and told myself to suck it up and be tough.

I remember staying up late watching the Olympics as a kid. I was hypnotized by the competitive spirit, the athletic prowess, and the laser-like focus. These athletes had worked a lifetime, and in a moment their dreams were fulfilled or broken. As a young boy, all I wanted was to be there—living out my dreams and winning the gold!

I discovered wrestling in middle school. As soon as I stepped onto the mat, I knew my life would never be the same again! It was the first time I felt like I belonged—like I was a part of something bigger than me. I wasn't very good at the beginning, but I loved the process of working hard and learning something new. Being a part of a team was exciting and it motivated me to keep going for it.

I began to think that wrestling just might be the ticket to my Olympic dream. By the time I was 15 years old, I was 4th in my weight class in the State of California! This qualified me for the Regional tournament in Bend, Oregon. It was part of the journey I needed to take to get a spot on the Olympic wrestling team someday.

I'll never forget the day I qualified for regionals—I was so pumped! For some reason, when my dad came to pick me up, I didn't say a word. All I could think about was how much this trip would cost. We didn't have much money, and my dad had sacrificed so much already just to get me to the many wrestling tournaments each Saturday. So I kept my mouth shut and, in that moment, I made a choice to pursue my dreams alone. I never allowed my dad, the rest of my family, my training partners, or my coach to be a part of my Olympic dream. I just kept my dream to myself.

I realized the lack of money was just an excuse. The real reason I didn't share my dream with anyone—the reason I pursued it alone— was *fear*. I was afraid to fail, and the easiest way to fail is to never really try at all. I finished my high school wrestling career quietly. I was the winningest wrestler on the team, but I fell far short of getting the college athletic scholarship I needed to continue the journey toward my Olympic dream.

A few years later during my senior year in college, I started coaching wrestling at a local high school. By the end of the season, my dream of being on the US Olympic Wrestling Team was reawakened, so I continued coaching and began training to win a spot on the team. I met and married my wife around this time and decided to share my dream with her. It was scary to be so vulnerable with someone. All those fearful thoughts came flooding back. What if I failed and my dream didn't come true? But I was amazed—my wife supported me unconditionally! Whether I won or lost didn't matter to her; she would still love me. Maybe I didn't have to pursue my dreams alone!

I wrestled in a Regional Olympic Qualifier and placed 3rd. I continued to coach and train for the next 4 years, but this time I wasn't alone. My wife supported me with kindness and encouragement.

Whenever I struggled, she stayed positive. I competed in my second Regional Olympic qualifier, but injured my right knee during practice just two days before. That knee was re-injured in my first match, so I 'injury-defaulted' out of the tournament. I thought back to high school and wondered if things would've worked out different if I'd shared my dream with my dad on that special day...the day I first qualified for regionals.

Do you remember the story of Daniel in the Lions' den? It's the story of how a lonely guy was placed in an even lonelier situation. Although he was a good Jew, Daniel found himself in Babylon, a captive and servant to the king of Babylon, Darius the Mede. Not only was Daniel a captive, but he was also born in captivity. Daniel never saw his homeland, but instead grew up as a stranger in a strange country. Daniel was alone.

To make matters worse, Daniel was found guilty of violating the king's laws by staying faithful to the one true God in prayer, and refusing to bow and pray to the king. As a punishment, the king had Daniel thrown into the den of lions, where he was sealed in by a large stone slab and left alone for the evening. In his loneliness, Daniel prayed to God, and God answered his prayer.

The next day the lions' den was opened back up, and the king called out to see if Daniel was still alive. Daniel responded, "My God sent his angel, and he shut the mouths of the lions. They have not hurt me, because I was found innocent in his sight."[1] Not only was Daniel released from the lions' den and restored to his position of authority, but the king ordered that all the people of Babylon "must fear and reverence the God of Daniel."[2]

Just like He did with Daniel, God sees the lonely in their loneliness. He understands their feelings, has compassion for them, and sends them help along the way. As a Campus Missionary, you can be like the angel God sent to keep Daniel company through the long night in the lions' den.

See Through the Loneliness

I kept my wrestling dreams to myself, and chose instead to be lonely, because I was afraid of failing. Oftentimes, when people choose to isolate themselves, it's not because they prefer loneliness, it's because something deeper is going on inside of them. You can be a blessing to the lonely by seeing through the loneliness, recognizing their uniqueness, and encouraging them in friendship.

Spend Time Together

If you know one of your friends is going through a time of loneliness, get involved by inviting him over to your house, or out to a meal. Do not judge him for his loneliness; feeling lonely is a perfectly normal part of being human. Instead, just spend time together without expectations. Don't try to fix the problem; being together is enough. As you earn his trust by spending time together and having conversations, he may eventually open up and share his heart with you.

Point to Jesus

Jesus knows what it's like to be lonely. On the cross, He experienced what might have been the loneliest point in His eternal existence. He cried out, "My God, my God, why have you abandoned me?"[3] In that moment, when Jesus had taken on all the sins of humanity, God the Father had to turn away and leave Him to die in loneliness. Think about that—not only did Jesus take on our sins, but he took on loneliness for us, as well. And ultimately, loneliness is cured through the peace that comes from knowing God and being fully surrendered to him. Point your lonely friends to Jesus by sharing His experience on the cross, and inviting them to begin conversing with God in prayer. God will answer them in their loneliness, and faith in Christ will not be far away.

Having a Conversation

You can help a lonely friend by having a conversation that can lead to Jesus. Here are some questions to get you started:

- **What's been going on lately? Tell me about it.** Ask them about their life. Take an interest in what's been going on. Sometimes people just need someone to talk to, and this question can also help you develop a good friendship.

- **What are you most excited about in the next month?** Generate hope for the future by asking them what they are looking forward to. This is a great optimistic conversation to have. When it's your turn to share, be certain to talk about the next youth event you are looking forward to and invite your friend to be a part of it.

- **What are your plans for this weekend?** This is a seemingly harmless question, but if they are lonely, it could be challenging for them. If they have plans, show some interest and ask them more questions. If they have no plans, you have an even greater opportunity. In that case, make a plan to spend time together or see if you can invite them to be a part of what you're doing.

- **Have you ever felt alone in a crowded room? What makes us feel this way?** Be sure to include yourself by saying "us" in the second question. Otherwise, it could sound like you are pointing out their loneliness as being unusual. Get right to the heart of the issue of loneliness by asking these questions. There may not be a right or wrong answer, and it's more important to listen to their feelings, anyway. Has there ever been a time in your life when you felt alone, but then God met you and took away your loneliness? Consider sharing that testimony with your friend.

- **Do you think God is aware of your life?** This is a great question to ask, and however they feel about it, you'll end up talking about God in this conversation. Most people really do believe God exists, and they often wonder if He hears their prayers or sees them in their loneliness. When it's appropriate, share Job 34:21 and Psalm 95:7. Give your perspective on God's love for all people, including the lonely. Pray together, and ask God to help each of you in times of loneliness.

---

[1] Daniel 6:22 NIV.
[2] Daniel 6:26 NIV.
[3] Matthew 27:46 ESV.

GOD
SO
LOVED.....

25

THE LONER

Ryan Goeden

The first day of school was usually great, but it always had the potential to be the worst. This was not because my classes were intimidating, or because I was worried about finding my way around the building, or because I was worried about people thinking my car was cool. No, the first day of school had the potential to be the worst because of one thing...lunch. Lunch was intimidating; not because I am vegan, or concerned what type of meat product went into my sloppy joe. Lunch had the potential to be the worst because, in the back of my mind, I was afraid I would end up sitting at the table by myself. Nothing at school scared me more than this.

The struggle was so incredibly real that as soon as I found out my lunch period, I would contact all my friends—from those I knew most to those I knew least. I needed to confirm that when I walked into that room full of happy people with all *their* friends, I could be seen as happy with all *my* friends too. I would play scenarios in my mind, trying to figure out what I would do if I could not find someone to sit with. This normally resulted in having lunch in the library alone, claiming to get in a "little extra study time."

Truth be told, I have never minded being alone. Most loners don't mind aloneness. Sometimes that's because we are used to it, and sometimes it's because it's simply our natural preference. My fear in those moments wasn't ever having time to myself, my fear always had to do with what people might think about me if I was the guy by myself. I was scared people would think things like, "He's a loser," or that I was the guy in a school with over 1000 people in it that couldn't find one person who cared enough to sit them. Even worse, I was afraid of picking up "pity friends" who would see me by myself and ask me to sit by them simply because of some social obligation, not because they felt I had anything to offer.

Every school has loners, and every school has students who are scared to be seen as a loner. In your school, several students are in this boat. We walk through the halls every day, wondering if anyone notices or cares. I would bet being alone at school is not the most difficult part of life for most of us, either. Most of us can deal with people we don't know not caring about us. Our real fear has to do with how we handle the questions we get at home. Questions like, "Who do you hang out with at school?" or "Why don't you go to the football game tonight?" or "Why don't you invite someone over this weekend?" We fear these questions because no one wants to tell their parents, for whatever reason, they don't fit in and they don't have very many, if any, good friends.

As I reflect on the evil in the world, there are all kinds of big things that come to mind: abortion, terrorism, poverty, and disease. Not to diminish any of those things, but it is also a great evil when someone who is made in God's image, created to do work for His Kingdom, would look at their life and feel worthless. Ephesians 2:10 says, *"For we are God's handiwork, created in Christ Jesus to do good works, which God prepared in advance for us to do."*[1] We also know, from the beginning of the world, that everything God made was commendable.[2] He has never made a mistake. Yet, real as that is, there are people in your school who see themselves as less than God's best. That is a lie from the enemy, but it rests in the hearts of students all over the world.

Seeing that evil prevail often leads people to ask the question: "Where is God?" If God cared so much why would he let people hurt so badly? There are many repercussions of a fallen world we do not have the space to get into, but suffice it to say, God still has a plan in every situation, and He has already intervened in a way that is constantly shaping culture around us.

God so loved the world that HE SENT his only Son.[3] God sent his Son to intervene in a world that was broken by sin. He did not simply end sin, because that would remove our free will completely. Instead, He sent His Son as the most powerful weapon to accomplish His will and purpose. When God sees brokenness, *He sends.* It is important to realize that Jesus was not coerced into going into the world—it was His choice. He chose to intervene in the lives of the broken, the hurting, the loner. He chose to help *us.* We can make the same choice today—to intervene to help those who feel alone, as though no one cares.

Never Condescend

Sometimes, when we see a person sitting alone, or someone has real and obvious struggles in life, we can think of ourselves as superior in some way or another. So we pity them, we feel bad for them, and then we treat them like they are somehow less than us. That is called "condescending." It means treating someone like they are below our dignity or importance. It's wrong, and not just because it's rude. It's wrong because the Scriptures teach us otherwise.

In Romans 3, Paul writes about the effect of sin, how it affects everyone and how we all fall short of God's glory. He writes, "There is no difference between Jew and Gentile, for all have sinned and fall short of the glory of God, and all are justified freely by his grace through the redemption that came by Christ Jesus."[4] Even if you could do everything in your life in a socially acceptable way, and be the most congenial person in your school, you still would not be good enough to be declared righteous in God's eyes. We all have sinned; we are all the same, there is no difference.

In God's eyes, you are the same as the loner. You are the same as the liar. You are the same as the cheater. You are the same as any other person you might be inclined to look down upon. No one is below your dignity to sit with or spend time with or to share Jesus with. So do not speak with, or look upon, the loner as though he or she is less than you. You are the same. Treat them as your social equal, because they are.

Take a Genuine Interest

Intervening means that God took an interest in us first. He did not wait for us to become interested in him before reaching out with love. The same can be said for the loner in your lunchroom. You, as God's love extended into the school campus, must take an interest in them first. Taking a genuine interest means more than sitting with them because you feel bad for them. It means sincerely becoming invested in getting to know them. It means sitting with them day-after-day, having many conversations week-after-week, until they become comfortable with you and can trust you. Remember, a lot of loners become that way because they are *used* to be being alone.

Become a Genuine Friend

Taking an interest at school is good, but becoming a genuine friend is better. What's the difference? Friendship doesn't end when the school bell rings at the end of the day. Friendship means inviting your new friend into your life. It means inviting them to your youth group and church outings, it means having them over to your house.

Remember this—God did not intervene in our lives because we were the "cool" kind of people He'd want to hangout with. That's ridiculous. Yet, that is same way many of us tend to treat people in social circles. We gravitate towards those who we believe are cool and that we would want to hangout with. Try taking on the attitude of Christ: in humility consider others better than yourself.[5] Become a genuine friend to the loner. Don't think about how it will change your social status, or what you'll get out of the relationship. Just be a good friend.

Having a Conversation

- **What's been the best part of your day so far? What makes it the best?** This is a good question just to show that you're interested. Listen closely, and let them know you care about their answer. You can also share the best part of your day if they ask.

- **Tell me a little about your family. What is your favorite part of your life at home?** Get to know the loner better. Start with their home life. They may be alone at school, but they are not alone at home.

- **What are some of your favorite things to do outside of school? What are your favorite hobbies?** Listen to their answers, because these are some great clues for building a stronger friendship. Find some common interests you can engage in together.

- **What are you most looking forward to this weekend?** See what their plans are, and see if there is any room to invite them into your weekend plans. Do you have a youth group activity for church on Sunday that you could invite them to?

- **What do you think about God? Do you think He is real?**
  You need to have a good relationship by the time you engage
  with this question. Loners aren't really alone, because the Holy
  Spirit speaks to everyone whether they know it or not.[6] There's
  a good chance they've thought about, or even talked to God in
  their alone times.

---

[1] NIV 2011.
[2] 1 Timothy 4:4.
[3] John 3:16.
[4] Romans 3:22b-24 NIV.
[5] Philippians 2:3.
[6] John 15:26, 16:28.

GOD SO LOVED....

26

THE POSER

George Volz

pos·er[1]

1. one who pretends to be someone whose not.
2. who tries to fit in but with exaggeration

Now...before you skip to the next chapter because you don't know any 'posers,' and you certainly aren't one, let's take a closer look. Can you honestly say, without hesitation, that you've never pretended to be someone you're not? I'm not referring to when you wrestle with siblings—acting like John Cena with off-the-couch body slams, or even taking your best selfie recording of "Halo" by Beyoncé—attempting to gain the same status as the famed performer. I'm talking about the attempt to fit in. With the same level of impersonation we use while playing make-believe, we may also attempt to fit in with a certain crowd or group. Do you know anyone like this? Do you find yourself in this definition?

If there were a High School Dictionary containing the word 'poser', it would probably have several sub-definitions of posers(with pictures included of course):

- The Skater poser—Usually seen wearing the newest Vans without a single scuff mark, and an extra long chain wallet.

- The Valley Girl poser, aka Plastics—Found in a seemingly endless selfie montage.

- The Redneck poser—Characterized by an entire wardrobe of Realtree camo, with as many leather accessories as possible.

Now please understand, there's nothing inherently wrong with having an interest or a style like the ones mentioned above. My point is this: we all like certain things or participate in certain things, and we do our best to fit in as we go. In this sense we all "pose" a little bit. However, when someone is trying his hardest to fit in somewhere, willing to go all in just to be accepted, he may just be a poser. We all want to be accepted, and being a poser is just one example of how we work towards that acceptance.

I remember a friend of mine in high school receiving his packed brown-bag lunch from his mom, followed by a kiss on the cheek as she saw him off for school. I may be exaggerating a little, but you get the idea. As he walked closer to the bus stop he would un-tuck his shirt, lower his pants, turn his hat sideways, and—the finishing touch—loosen his boot laces and fold the tongue out. Now he was ready to enter "the pack!" Honestly, if his parents had returned to bring him something he'd forgotten, they probably wouldn't have recognized him! Do you know anyone like this?

I discovered I was a poser in high school. I was with a group of my friends (my regular friends), when one of my 'non-regular' friends came over with some of his crew. After greeting them and talking for a bit, they began to walk away. That's when one of the regulars asked, "What the heck was that?"

I replied emphatically, "What the heck was what?"

He shot back, "Since when do you use 'nah-mean' in your vocabulary?!"[2]

That's when I realized that I only used "nah-mean" when I was with that other group of friends. It was then that I began to contemplate which 'me' was the real me. I had always thought, "I am who I am. Nobody forces me to do anything I don't want to do. Just cause I roll with them, it doesn't mean I'm like them." That was what I believed, but my behavior showed otherwise. The truth is *we are* influenced by those around us. Sometimes this happens naturally as we spend time together. Other times we pose because we are desperate for acceptance.

Let's take a look at some interesting words the Apostle Paul wrote about himself:

> No man has any hold on me, but I have made myself a workman owned by all. I do this so I might lead more people to Christ. I became as a Jew to the Jews so I might lead them to Christ. There are some who live by obeying the Jewish Law. I became as one who lives by obeying the Jewish Law so I might lead them to Christ. There are some who live by not obeying the Jewish law. I became as one who lives by not obeying the Jewish law so I might lead them to Christ. This does not mean that I do not obey God's Law. I obey the teachings of Christ. Some are weak. I have become weak so I might lead them to Christ. I have become like every person so in every way I might lead some to Christ. Everything I do, I do to get the Good News to men. I want to have a part in this work.[3]

Did we just read that correctly? Did Paul basically just label himself a poser? If you were to read all of Paul's writings, I believe you'd conclude that Paul was actually living out the life God had intended for him: to preach the message of salvation to all kinds of people. In order to fulfill this call, Paul was willing to change little things about himself in order to fit in, so that he could better communicate the message of salvation. He wasn't willing to sin, but he was willing to change. You may think he was a poser, but in reality, he was taking a sincere interest in the lifestyles and habits of others, so that he could find the best way to earn their trust, share the gospel, and disciple them as followers of Christ. These circumstances were placed before Paul, and Paul owned each one so that he could be a credible witness to whomever he was with.

In a sense, we are all called to be posers. In the book of Ephesians, also written by Paul, he tells us to be "imitators of God."[4] Of course, our call to imitate God involves so much more than being a poser. We not only strive to love as God loves, we strive to do so in everything. We don't just want to show God's love with "the regulars," we want to show God's love to everyone, everywhere. This is where acceptance is truly found—in the love of our Creator. And we are fulfilled when we are fully committed to Him.

Be An Imitator of God

Don't look down on others, or yourself, for being a poser. Instead, remember that posing is ultimately a search for acceptance, and ultimate acceptance and fulfillment is found in a commitment to Jesus Christ. Become the person the Holy Spirit is calling you to be, an imitator of God, by becoming a friend to those who pose, those who don't fit in, and others who may just be searching for acceptance. Start a conversation with them, and earn their trust so that you can share the Gospel.

Invite and Celebrate

Demonstrate acceptance and love by inviting the posers, those who don't quite fit in, and those longing for acceptance to your church or youth group. Welcome them and celebrate them with love and eagerness! Consider hosting a "melting pot" event and invite all types of people, no matter the stereotype. Make it a blast! Invite them to bring their favorite food/snack/candy to show the similarities that we all have in common. This could be a karaoke night with prop and wardrobe attire so everyone can be a poser for a song. This would be a great opportunity to share how God loves everyone, no matter how we look or what we like. Or make it a coffee house style night, with an open mic where everyone can share and express their uniqueness.

Having a Conversation

The first step in sharing the Gospel with a poser is taking an interest in them by having a conversation. Here are some great questions to get you started:

- **What are you most interested in? Tell me about it.** Take an interest in them! In this way you can help them to feel accepted.

- **Who did you 'make believe' most often when you were a child? How far did you take it (costume, voice, secret hideout)?** This is just an interesting conversation topic. It will help you to get to know them better.

- **Oftentimes I find myself acting differently at home than I do at school. How about you? Where do you reveal your genuine self more, at home or at school?** Admitting that we all behave a little differently in different places is good. It will help your friend or conversation partner become more comfortable in seeing this behavior in himself.

- **Have you ever found your interests changing from year to year, or from Middle School to High School? Do we make those changes on our own? Or do others influence us? Is either way right or wrong?** Don't judge the poser; instead ask this question in an open and honest way. There's really no right or wrong answer here, so let them answer for themselves. Give your opinion if asked.

- Share 1 Corinthians 9:19-23 with your new friend. Then ask, **"Like Paul, Do you find yourself adapting to certain groups, yet continuing your true inner self? Or do you find imitating a particular group on the outside first (fashion, speech, etc) changes your inner self also?"** There is a great connection here to the Gospel. Whatever answers your friend gives, you can discuss it and also bring Paul's words back into the conversation. Talk about his motivation for changing himself—that everyone should know Jesus. Take a risk and share the Gospel with your friend now.

---

[1] www.urbandictionary.com.

[2] "nah-mean" is slang for, "Know what I mean?"

[3] 1 Corinthians 9:19-23 NLT.

[4] Ephesians 5:1-2 NLT.

GOD
SO
LOVED....

27

STUDENTS WHO NEVER FEEL GOOD ENOUGH

Tom Bachman and the Oregon Youth Alive Ministry Academy Students

To most people, if they'd looked at his home life, everything was in perfect order. If you were a neighbor, you wouldn't have heard any yelling. You wouldn't have seen people coming home at late hours, too much drinking, or anything that seemed out of place. In fact, you would notice that every Sunday morning this family pulled out of their driveway at 9am and were back home at 12:30pm. They appeared to be the perfect church-going family. This young man might have even been called "privileged." He had a Mom and Dad, both of whom had jobs, three siblings, and the family had nice cars. Everything seemed just right on the outside. However, inside the home, it was a silent mess.

While Mom was loving, caring, and often complementing—Dad was not. The young son was always trying to please his dad. He played an instrument that his dad played. He tried to be in the sports that his

177

dad participated in during high school. He joined Boy Scouts just to accumulate the things his dad seemed to value. His older brother was more athletic, more successful in playing the instruments, and he even had completed his Eagle Scout—just like Dad. So when Dad's approval didn't come for the youngest son, when the love that he so desperately wanted never came, he began to do other things that he thought might gain recognition and approval.

Everything he tried became successful, only to have his father stare blankly back with no approval. There was even a day early on that this young man made a life commitment to gaining his father's approval and love. With this commitment, he became driven to be accepted by all those around him, which in many cases pushed others in his diverse world away. He had few friends, The athletes in school made fun of him because he was not good at sports. Instead, he was good at grades and singing, but no one seemed to notice.

When he grew up, the same patterns plagued this man throughout his life. He became a workaholic, just like his Dad. However, instead of gaining his Dad's approval it seemed his father still didn't care. This man spent a majority of his life trying to please others only to live a dark life of feeling like he was *never good enough*. This life of feeling never good enough has turned into trying to be accepted by others at all costs. It has led to the accidental training of his own kids to live their lives by working for the approval of others. It has led to depression and anxiety, not because of the actions of others, but due to his own low self-esteem and a lifetime of comparing himself to others.

You may not know by looking at the students in your school, but many of them also suffer from feeling like they are not good enough. These students are everywhere, and if you will take the time to notice them and get involved, you can make a huge difference in their lives and in the Kingdome of God.

Moses was born to a family that was living in slavery in another country. This is not normal for today, but for generations this was a normal experience for many people. We see this as being born in the midst of a terrible situation, but Moses and his family would have seen it as normal. The ruler of the slaves and the country, Pharoah, was threatened by the growing slave population. He decided to carry out genocide; to murder all of the male children of the slaves. Moses was a newborn baby, and his mom loved him so much that she worked to try to save his life. She put Moses in a basket and floated him down the river, where he was found by Pharoah's daughter.

Pharoah's daughter decided to keep Moses. He was raised in privilege—in the royal house—but was always different because he was from the race of slaves. He was raised with a great education, yet his own race disowned him. He may have found himself in a place of never meeting the expectations of anyone. When he tried to make a great choice for justice by saving a slave's life, he ended up killing the guard who was beating the slave. This likely made his self-esteem crumble even more.

In the midst of this, God spoke to him and called him out. By this time his self-esteem was so fragile that he made excuses of why God couldn't use him. Moses believed he couldn't speak well enough. Moses believed his own people wouldn't see him as a good enough leader. Moses came up with excuse after excuse, believing lie after lie, until low self-esteem ruled his life (Exodus 4:1,10,13). Finally, Moses surrendered his issues of self-esteem to God. When he did so, Moses became a leader driven to be obedient to the true Father, the Heavenly Father. This transformation took him to a time of growth in the desert. It was in the desert that God began to grow Moses into the leader that was needed during his time. It was here that he realized that God would be with him and strengthen him, and that God was going to be his "enough." Moses didn't have to be good enough anymore, God was the one who was enough for Moses. Moses went on to set his people free from slavery through God's guidance and power.

Slow Down and Take Notice

Perhaps you've had a life of trying to live up to someone else's expectations. If so, you may fall into this same self-esteem issues— always trying to be what you assume others want out of you. Even when you think you have achieved what they want, you yourself may suffer through the lie that you will never be good enough. *You are the exact person that God is looking to help*, and God also wants to help those in your school or your friend group who suffer from the same thing. If this is you, you will more easily recognize others who are hurting throughout your daily routine.

Even if you don't suffer from low self-esteem, you can still recognize those who do. They may be sitting in the lunch room alone, they may be the loud mouth in a classroom, they may be the bully or the bullied, they may be the class clown, the best athlete, the sports team manager, the overachiever, or the underachiever. These kinds of personality traits could be the result of trying to fit in and gain someone else's approval. If you want to serve and share Jesus with those who experience low self-esteem, you've got to slow down and notice these people in your life.

Create an Environment of Love and Acceptance

Once you've slowed down and taken notice, begin to ask tons of questions and never quit caring! It is in this type of environment, which you can create, that people experience the opportunity to be real and to feel accepted. You can create an environment of love and acceptance that makes them feel like they fit in for the first time in their lives. In this environment you can unseat—even if just for a moment—the negative feeling and behavior that is a pattern for those with low self-esteem.

Even if you personally experience low self-esteem and a feeling of never being good enough, you can create an environment of love and acceptance. God has already given you what you need to do this. God will turn your weakness into strength if you trust Him. You must be willing to walk together with those experiencing these issues. In fact, God may be asking you to walk with them, even in your own weakness.

Be a Good Friend

Those who are drowning in the lie of never being good enough need good friends. They need friends who will accept them just like they are. They need friends that will listen and not compare themselves to the other person. They need friends that listen and repeat back what they heard them say. They need friends that don't always have the answer, but are empathetic to the pain. They need friends that invite them to their home where your parents may show them unconditional love and acceptance. They need friends that will eat with them, hang out with them, and never quit on them.

Be a Friend Who Points to Jesus

Those with low self-esteem don't just need good friends, they need godly friends who will point them to Jesus. They need friends that pray with them. They need friends that hurt with and suffer hardships with them. They need friends that encourage and point out, over and over, the God-given beauty of their character and giftings. They need friends that are willing to walk with them thru Scriptures of who God says that they are (Child of God, chosen generation, royal priesthood, etc.). They need friends that think more of others than they do of themselves. They need a friend who will show them that "God so loved" by showing them God's love and sharing Jesus with them

Having a Conversation

Asking questions about their life and being very interested in the small details will help your friends to trust you. As you listen quietly, ask God for your next question and ask God to help you be all that He wants you to be. Most of all, be aware that you don't want these new friends just to shut down. Take your time. A friendship is not a sprint, it is a marathon.

- **What are some of your favorite things? What about your least favorite things?**
- **What is your biggest hope in life? What is your biggest dream?**
- **What are your biggest challenges and hurts?**
- **What do you believe God thinks about you?**
- **How do you believe God feels about you?**

GOD
SO
LOVED....

<u>28</u>

TRANSGENDER STUDENTS

Linda Seiler

From my earliest memory, I wanted to be a boy instead of a girl. I didn't want to wear dresses or play with dolls like my older sister. I wanted to shave and mow the lawn like Dad. My parents thought I was a tomboy and that it was a phase I'd outgrow but it was no phase for me. I was obsessed with being a boy and even prayed as a child that God would change me into a boy.

In grade school, I heard there was such a thing as a "sex change operation" (known today as gender affirmation surgery). I determined that as soon as I was old enough and had enough money, I would change my name to David, get a sex change, and live happily ever after.

As I entered junior high, and all the other girls around me were experimenting with makeup and wanting to date boys, I found myself repulsed by my body that was beginning to show signs of womanhood. I became intensely jealous of the boys around me, whose voices were changing, and they were becoming everything I longed to be. Around the same time, I discovered that I was attracted to women.

I didn't choose that.
I didn't want that.
But I felt helpless to change it.

Nobody talked about LGBTQ matters when I grew up in the 1980's, so I felt like I had to keep it all to myself and figure out life on my own. I reasoned that if I was really a male trapped inside a female body, I should be attracted to women. That would've just made me a straight male. I decided I needed to hold out until I could get the sex change, and then my world would make sense.

As I neared high school, I started to think through my plan in greater detail. How would I tell my family? What would my parents think? What would the neighbors think? What would my *grandparents* think? I couldn't bear the thought being rejected, so I figured I only had two options: a) run away, have the "sex change," and live happily ever after without seeing my family again, or b) don't have the surgery, keep my family, and do my best to fit in so that no one would ever know my deep, dark secret.

I remember the moment I consciously chose option b. I didn't have any friends at school, and I figured my family was all I had. I didn't want to go through life alone, even if it meant I got to "become" a man.

From that point forward, I decided to "dress the part" so that no one would ever know my internal struggle. I grew my hair out and tried to dress more like a girl. I tried dating boys, hoping that would "awaken" attractions to the opposite sex. That didn't work. It only made me more intensely jealous of men. I wanted to be the man with the woman, not the woman with the man.

My junior year in high school, I surrendered my life to Jesus and thought all my struggles would disappear now that I was saved. However, I found myself still attracted to women and desiring to be a man. Throughout high school and college, I kept my secret to myself, lest I be rejected by my Christian friends.

I did my best to follow Christ during college, but my secret continued to gnaw at me. I found myself sexually attracted to women who were discipling me, and I was enslaved to private sexual addictions. I was a leader in my college ministry group, and it looked like I had it all together—but inside I was miserable. My senior year, I heard a message about getting free from repeated sin, and the speaker said the key was James 5:16, "Confess your sins to each other and pray for each other so that you may be healed." I don't remember anything else the speaker said. All I knew was that I'd never be free until I brought my secret into the light with a trusted leader.

I expected my campus pastor to condemn me when I confessed all to him, but instead he commended me for taking a risk to tell him my struggles, and he said he would get me the help that I needed. That was the first step in the journey of transformation in my life. Over time, the Lord revealed why I believed the lie that it's superior to be a man than a woman, and He healed my heart from deep wounds of rejection and wrong views of women. Those wounds contributed to my desire to be a man and to my attractions to women.

I'm now decades removed from the first time I confessed my struggles to my campus pastor, and the Lord has brought such deep healing to my heart that I no longer believe being a woman is inferior. By God's grace, I'm able to embrace my womanhood and enjoy who God created me to be. As I continued to walk out my healing, I eventually began to experience attractions to men—which I never dreamed would happen. (Note: not everyone who struggles with their gender identity experiences attractions to the same sex, but both transgender desires and same-sex attractions are rooted in feelings of rejection.)

If you or someone you love struggles with their gender identity, there's hope in Jesus. He can reveal the wounds in our heart that the father of lies (Satan) uses to convince us that our birth sex is inferior and that "becoming" the opposite sex would be better. The truth is, God knit us each together in our mother's womb, and we are fearfully and wonderfully made in God's image as male and female (Psalm 139, Genesis 1). Just as the clay can't say to the potter, "You don't know what you're doing," so we can't say to God, "You made a mistake when you created my biological sex" (Isaiah 45:9). God has amazing plans for us in the sex He created us to be. It's Satan who tries to convince us otherwise, and he most often uses wounds of rejection to convince us that "becoming" the opposite sex will bring us the affirmation we desire. It won't. Only Jesus can fill our thirst for love and affirmation.

Serving Your Transgender Friend

The best way you can serve your friend who struggles with their gender identity is not to affirm them in a false identity (calling a boy a girl or vice versa), but to affirm their unique personality temperament and natural talents that God gave them when He knit them together in the womb. Gender dysphoria (being unhappy with one's biological sex) is most often rooted in feelings of rejection and believing that becoming the opposite sex will give them worth (which is a lie). Instead of agreeing with a lie, ask God for creative ways to affirm how your friend has been fearfully and wonderfully made.

For example, many times, a boy who struggles with gender dysphoria doesn't fit traditional male stereotypes (rough-and-tumble, athletic, loves sports and the outdoors, etc.). Instead, he may have a sensitive temperament and be gifted in the arts, theatre, or music. That male friend needs to know that being in touch with his emotions is beautiful (even Jesus wept) and that his gifts as an artist, actor, or musician are valued. He needs male friends who will affirm him as a man among men. He is not a lesser male simply because his gifts don't fit a cultural stereotype.

Conversely, girls who have strong personalities and are gifted in athletics can sometimes feel like they don't fit in and may struggle with their gender identity. Such girls need to be affirmed by their female peers as a woman among women, even though their interests may differ from what our culture traditionally calls "feminine."

These days, it's common for teenage girls who have never doubted their biological sex to adopt a nonbinary or trans identity because they believe the lie that an alternative identity will make life more bearable. The decision to "transition" is usually rooted in feelings of rejection. Again, the best thing you can do for your friend is not to affirm them in a false identity but to affirm them as the amazing person God created them to be.

Having a Conversation

Get to know your friend by spending time with them and building trust. Find an activity they enjoy and offer to do it with them. Take a genuine interest in them and don't treat them like a project. Remember, your friend is likely dealing with wounds of rejection, and they need to know they are loved for who they are. Their greatest problem is not that they struggle with their gender identity; their greatest problem is that they don't know Jesus. As you build relationship, pray the Lord will give you opportunities to talk to your friend about Jesus. Below are some questions you can ask when you have built a friendship based on trust:

- **Tell me more about your journey with your gender identity. When did you first feel like being the opposite sex would be desirable? What was that like? Who was the first person you told? How did they respond?** (Empathize with your friend and try to relate to the pain and rejection they may be feeling.)
- **What do you find undesirable about your birth sex?**
- **What do you admire most about the opposite sex?** (The answer to this and the above question can sometimes reveal wounds in the heart and where the person has felt rejected or like a failure in their birth sex.)
- **If God were to enter the room right now and look your direction, what do you think His facial expression and body language would be?** (Those who struggle with their sexuality often feel like God condemns them, and their answer to this question may reveal that and provide opportunity to talk about what God is really like.)

Would you consider coming with me to church sometime? God loves you and wants to reveal Himself to you.

GOD SO LOVED....

<u>29</u>
AGNOSTICS

Andy Lynn

It was about 10:30pm on a Friday night, and we were hanging out with a group of juniors and seniors after a church service; the custodians had already begun cleaning around us when the conversation went pretty deep. The circle was discussing their frustrations, doubts, and questions about church and I could see tears building in one of the girl's eyes. Her name was Ashley. She wasn't saying much the whole time, but she blurted out what she couldn't hold in any longer with such honesty and sincerity. "I'm just not sure how we can know for sure that the Christian God is the right choice!!!... How can we know for sure that what we believe is true???"

Her fear, doubt, and shame were now visible to all. I smiled at her and said, "Being an agnostic is not a bad place to be... it's actually a great starting point."

"I'm sorry...What did you call me?!?!" she asked.

I laughed and told her that an agnostic is someone who does not believe there is enough evidence to prove if there is or isn't a God and whether a specific faith should be followed.

"I am so excited for you!!!" I said as she sat on the multi-purpose room floor. She had a perplexed look in her eyes as she wiped the post-cry and makeup mixture off of her face.

"Excited? Why is that?" she said with curiosity.

"Agnostics are on a search for truth, and we are promised in Jeremiah 29:13 that 'if we seek God with all of our heart that we will find Him.'[1] The exciting part," I told her, "is that if you seek God with everything you have, then you will find Him. How cool is that? You are about to have an encounter with God!" She seemed less excited than I was. Spoiler Alert: Her journey of seeking Jesus would take her almost 2 years, but she encountered Him for herself just like Thomas in 2021!!!! Ashley went from having no concrete belief or faith—also called being a "none"—to having solid faith in Jesus. Let's look at how to help others like Ashley move from doubt and fear to belief and a hope!

Researchers are using the term "nones" to describe the recent growth in agnostics from the latest census numbers because they are choosing "no religious affiliation" when asked what religion they belong to. Atheism, Christianity, Judaism, and Islam are all selections, but they are choosing "no religious affiliation. That's where the nickname comes from—they are the non-religions, the nones.[2]

The fastest growing faith in the United States as of the printing of this book is agnosticism or nones. Over 29% of Americans consider themselves to be agnostic or non-religious according to the 2021 Pew Research Study which is up from 16% in 2007.[3] According to Pew Research, this means they are the largest and most common mission field (by belief) in the U.S.

You may not hear someone label themselves as an agnostic, but the typical agnostic will say things like this:

- "I believe there is a higher power, but who knows which one is right?"
- "If the God of the Bible loves me like you say, why doesn't He make it clear?"
- "Who can know for sure what is right and what is wrong?"

There is often confusion between the terms atheism and agnosticism. A famous agnostic, Bertrand Russel, was often asked if being agnostic was similar to being an atheist and he would explain, "No. An atheist, like a Christian, holds that we can know whether or not there is a God. The Christian holds that we can know there is a God; the atheist, that we can know there is not. The Agnostic suspends judgment, saying that there are not sufficient grounds either for affirmation or for denial."[4] Agnostics are the doubters, the skeptics, and we even see them in scripture with people like Thomas.

After the resurrection, Thomas was the only disciple who had not yet seen Jesus with his own eyes. In John 20:25 we see Thomas frustrated with doubt and refusing to believe unless He sees Jesus for Himself. So, the other disciples tell him, "We have seen the Lord," attempting to convince Thomas.

Thomas replied, "Unless I see in his hands the mark of the nails, and place my finger into the mark of the nails, and place my hand into his side, I will never believe."[5]

Thomas traveled with Jesus and still had doubt about His resurrection until He encountered Jesus for himself after Jesus had risen from the dead. Agnostics want to see Jesus for themselves. Some of them may even be in your youth group, and they feel shame and guilt because of their doubts. Jesus came and met Thomas in the middle of his doubts and unbelief, and He will do the same for your friends and circles of influence.

Do you know agnostics in your school? Do you know agnostics in your family? Take a moment and write down the names of some of the agnostics you know:

_____   _____

_____   _____

We do not have the power to save anyone. Let's say that one more time...we don't have the power to save anyone. Jesus loves the individual far more than we ever will and desires their salvation more than we could ever imagine. In John 15 Jesus uses a parable of a vineyard to help us understand the process. Jesus says that God is the vineyard owner, and Jesus is the vine that sustains us (the branches). We have one job to do—to trust in Jesus and that He will use us to bear fruit or to make disciples. We can't take credit for the fruit; the fruit belongs to the vineyard owner (God) and the vine (Jesus).

Share Jesus through your Abilities and Interests.

When Jesus said, "Follow me and I will make you a fisher of men."[5] He was talking to fishermen, if he was talking to you I think he would say follow me and I will take your abilities and interests to reach your agnostic friends. There is a simple way that we can open up a conversation with an agonistics, and that is to attribute our good game, good grades, our success, our peace, or our joy to Jesus versus our circumstances. This could be on social media where we thank God for His peace in a tough week, or when someone asks us about our success or talents. Instead of just saying, "Thanks I worked hard...," we can say the truth with a statement like, "I am so thankful that God allows me to use my gifts to show my love for Him and others." Agnostics will normally ask questions to understand how we can "know," and it allows us to share our testimony and challenge or encourage them on their search for truth.

Pray for your Agnostic Friends

Prayer is the most powerful weapon we have in evangelism, and this is especially true with our agnostic friends. When I first meet an agnostic I ask them if I can pray for them in anyway, so far I have never been told, "no." Most people—even agnostics—hope that God or some form of higher power is hearing them. Oftentimes, asking what they could use prayer for opens the door for us to serve them in some way, or least care for them in friendship. When we pray for them we get to be an intercessor, which means to pray on behalf of someone or to "stand in the gap." Pray for them by name. Ask God to reveal Himself to them, and to use you in any way to speak truth. Pray for opportunities to talk openly about your experience with Jesus, His Spirit, or the church.

Encourage the Search for Truth

Remember, agnostics believe that we can't prove God's existence, but you are walking proof to the agnostic when you share your experiences and encounters with God. If the agnostic was the jury in a courtroom, we often put the pressure on ourselves to be the lawyer to prove our case. But we aren't the lawyer who has a case; we are simply the witness sharing what we have seen and experienced. The witness doesn't control the outcome; they just report the truth from their perspective. Always encourage an Agnostic's search for truth. I have witnessed dozens of agnostics search for Jesus and find Him as scripture encourages anyone to do. I usually challenge them to seek the truth and ask God to reveal Himself. Some who loves truth has nothing to lose by testing God in this way. Start today by having a conversation with an agnostic friend about an experience you had with God. Share how your faith helps guide you or gives you hope. Ask God to give you this opportunity!

Having a Conversation

Agnostics by definition are full of uncertainty. They are unsure that any truth is able to be obtained.[6] So, one great conversation you can have with an agnostic is on the subject of truth. Specifically, you can explore the question, "What is truth?" Instead of trying to convince the agnostic of your perspective, pull a play from Jesus' playbook and ask questions that allow you to jump into their worldview. A great resource for questions is Dare2Share.org, and below are some great starter questions they recommend specifically for agnostics.[7] Ask one of these questions to a friend and just listen. If you are asked to give your opinion, by all means talk about God and share your own thoughts and experiences.

- **Have you had any sort of religious background?**
- **How did you arrive at the spiritual place you find yourself now?**
- **Do you ever secretly wish you could know for sure that there was a God who loved you?**
- **What would "proof" for God's existence look like to you?**
- **Are there things you believe in that have not been proven to you?**
- **Do you think people are basically good? How do you explain the presence of evil in the world?**
- **Have you ever thought about the possibility that you might be wrong about what you believe about God?** (Be ready to answer this question yourself!)

---

[1] ESV

[2] "About Three-in-Ten U.S. Adults Are Now Religiously Unaffiliated." Pew Research Center, Religion and Public Life, accessed April 27, 2022, (https://www.pewresearch.org/religion/2021/12/14/about-three-in-ten-u-s-adults-are-now-religiously-unaffiliated/).

[3] Ibid.

[4] "Am I an atheist or an agnostic?" Russel, Bertrand (1947) accessed on April 27, 2022 https://scepsis.net/eng/articles/id_6.php.

[5] ESV

[6] "Agnostic," Dictionary.com, accessed April 28, 2021, http://dictionary.reference.com/browse/agnostic.

[7] "How to share the Gospel with an atheist," Dare2Share Ministries, accessed on April 27, 2022 https://www.dare2share.org/worldviews/agnostics/.

GOD

SO

LOVED....

30
ATHEISTS
Bradly Keller and Lee Rogers[1]

Gil grew up in a family that attended church once in a while. He heard some things about tradition and being religious, but never thought that any of it applied to him. When he was 13 years old, he told his parents that he no longer wanted to go to church. So instead of attending services, Gil was allowed to stay home. He felt free—no longer having to go thru the motions and rituals, no longer fighting boredom as he listened to someone recite a reading. He grew up to become a "happy" young adult atheist. He went to a good college, got a good job, and was generally happy living life on his own terms.

While on a vacation with his brother he met a girl who believed in God (not making her the smartest person in his book). Despite their differences, they started a long distance relationship. Gil was determined to show her that being religious and believing in God was irrational. In his opinion, she needed to put this absurd belief behind her so they could get on with their relationship. This was an important moment for Gil. He knew many intelligent people who didn't believe in God, yet they seemed to base their disbelief on flimsy assumptions. Gil was looking for something stronger—a rational argument to disprove God's existence.

Gil didn't think he could disprove Christianity without knowing what it professed to believe. So he opened up a bible and began to read it for himself, trying to figure out a way to prove God wasn't real. He came up with an experiment to disprove Christianity—prayer. He prayed, "If there is a God, then here I am. I'm looking into this. Why don't you go ahead and reveal yourself to me? I'm open."

While reading the Bible he was struck by the authority with which Jesus spoke. He was also impressed by Jesus' handling of some very powerful and intelligent people of the time. The people who followed Jesus, even though they suffered for speaking of Christ's death and resurrection, fascinated him. But he still wasn't ready to change his view of God.

Instead, he tried another experiment, this time it was going to church. He went to church like he was going to an art gallery; just there to observe, take it all in, and leave. He was uncomfortable, sitting there thinking to himself, "What if my friends or family saw me in here?" Still, he sat thru all of the service and was ready to leave. He was walking out the door when something stopped him—something was nagging at him. "I have to figure this all out," he thought to himself.

Gil stopped, turned around, approached the pastor, and asked him about Jesus. The pastor took Gil to his office, said a short prayer, and began to answer the many questions Gil had. Over the next several weeks he continued to meet with this pastor, asking question after question. The pastor was clearly educated and took the time to answer his questions. Gil took pages and pages of notes over the course of their meetings. There was one question that kept distressing him: "Why did Jesus have to die? That's when Gil experienced what 2 Corinthians 7:10 calls "godly sorrow."

Gil, while never a "bad" person, had done something that was out of character. He had chosen to go against what he knew to be right and had done something outside the bounds of morality, as he understood it. He felt terrible about it. The results of his decision were guilt and shame like he had never experienced. Gil lie awake for sleepless nights, trying to rationalize it away in his mind. Then the realization came—this is why Jesus had to die! Jesus took the penalty that Gil was supposed to face. Jesus carried the guilt and shame so that Gil wouldn't have to. In that moment, Gil gave his life to Jesus Christ.

Many Christians picture atheists as evil people with no moral center. To be sure, there have been some atheists who were downright evil[2], but there have also been Christians who did evil while claiming to follow God. Is it possible to be good apart from God? For Gil, the answer was yes, and you probably know some atheists who are good people, too. But what does it mean to be good? The concepts of right and wrong are universal to humanity, and in spite of the differences among various cultures there is a universal recognition that certain values pertain to all mankind. So where does the idea of right and wrong come from? Where does the concept of good and evil come from? Atheism cannot answer this question.

A second failure of atheism is that science fails to answer many questions as it relates to the earth and the universe. The Big Bang theory, for example, can explain how the universe came to exist in its current state, but it cannot explain the cause or the origin of the energy behind the "bang." A third failure is that atheism fails to address the deep questions of human existence such as, "Why do I exist? What is my purpose?" and "Where does hope come from?"

In Romans 1-2, the Apostle Paul makes the case that it's possible to know about God even if you've never been told about God or read about Him in the Bible. These are great verses to discuss with atheists. In Romans 1:18-19 he wrote, "For what can be known about God is plain to them, because God has shown it to them. For his invisible attributes, namely, his eternal power and divine nature, have been clearly perceived, ever since the creation of the world, in the things that have been made. So they are without excuse."[3] Paul's first piece of logic was nature; the earth, the universe, and the human being. Paul believed that the clockwork nature of the universe couldn't have happened by accident; God must have designed it.

The second point Paul makes is in Romans 2:14-15, "For when Gentiles, who do not have the law, by nature do what the law requires, they are a law to themselves, even though they do not have the law. They show that the work of the law is written on their hearts, while their conscience also bears witness..."[4] His second piece of logic was the human conscience; the idea that almost all humans know what right and wrong are and feel badly when they do not do the right thing. Paul was saying that men know what right and wrong are naturally, and that doesn't happen by accident; a Creator imprints it upon their minds.

These two points, nature and conscience, are the two key questions to engage in when trying to discuss God's existence: What makes the universe work so well? What causes the sense of right and wrong in us?

Live On Purpose

If you want to share Jesus with an atheist, you've got to live your life on purpose. In everything you do, let people know you are a Christian. Let them see it in your life, in your kindness, in your integrity. Opening a door to Jesus can begin when people see Him through your day-to-day actions, attitudes, and behaviors. You don't have to be perfect—that's impossible, so don't even try. But you do have to walk with humility, apologizing when you're wrong, and treating everyone like they are your brother or sister.

Pray Like it Depends On God

There's an old saying, "Pray like everything depends on God, but work like everything depends on you."[5] We'll adapt that saying just a little bit for our purposes here, but we'll keep the first part the same: pray like sharing Jesus with your atheist friend depends entirely on God. In a way, it does. The Holy Spirit gives us words to say, God can orchestrate circumstances to give you an opportunity, and He can soften the heart of any atheist. You must continually make your atheist friend a matter of prayer, and you must ask God sincerely to help you and to prepare you to have a great conversation.

Study Like it Depends On You

God will help us as we pray, but it's also expected that we do our part in approaching an atheist friend for a conversation about Jesus. This chapter gives a very small glimpse into the discussions and conversations you could be having with an atheist. There really is so much more information, and much more detail, that you could be studying and using to engage your atheist friend in meaningful conversation. Many sincere atheists are quite intelligent, and they will appreciate being able to discuss God's existence with someone who approaches the issue with the same intellectual vigor as they do. Research and study "Intelligent Design Theory" and "Natural Moral Law" to find more points of conversation and discussion.

Having a Conversation

Every good conversation begins and flows with good questions. Here are some questions to get you going, but you can always develop your own and allow the conversation to flow naturally:

- **Have you ever wondered if God is real?** It's okay to start here, especially if you've got a good friendship and you've been active in the other conversations. They may say no, or they may say something that offends you, but that's okay. Just listen! Get them talking about God. Follow up with, *"Why do you feel that way?"*

- **Do you think much about spiritual things?** This can open the door to a lot of good conversations. The "spiritual" world is broad, so also remember that you may be opening up a can of worms. They may talk about ghosts, or card readers, or angels and demons. That's okay, just get them talking about spirituality. Even a conversation about ghosts points to the existence of the supernatural, and God himself is supernatural. When the opportunity comes in the conversation, just say, *"What about God? Do you think there is a God?"*

- **How is it possible for the universe to work together so well?** This is a great conversation that's been had all through history by philosophers and theologians. In short, the clockwork nature of creation points to a "clockmaker."

- **What made it possible for me to know right and wrong when I was a kid, before anyone taught me?** This is another great conversation that philosophers have had for millennia. You can read more about it in the rest of this chapter, and we've already talked about it a little bit. Get them thinking about the nature of morality. *Where does morality come from?*

---

[1] Portions of this chapter are taken from Chapter 9 of *Initiate: Powerful Conversations That Lead to Jesus* (Createspace: 2014).

[2] Two of the most noted atheists who were downright evil include Joseph Stalin and Mao Zedong. Stalin is believed to have killed 34-49 milion Russians who opposed him in some way from 1928-1954. Mao killed 45 million Chinese in just four years, from 1958-1962. Sources: Iosif G. Dyadkin, *Unnatural Deaths in the USSR, 1928-1954* (New Brunswick: Transaction Books, 1983), and Frank Dikötter, *Mao's Great Famine* (New York: Walker & Co., 2010), x.

[3] ESV.

[4] ESV.

[5] No one is really certain where this saying comes from, and some modern authors have used it in their writing. Some people attribute this saying to Saint Augustine, but the likely source is Ignatius of Loyola, who lived from 1491-1556. He wrote, "There is no need to wear yourself out, but make a competent and sufficient effort, and leave the rest to him who can do all he pleases." Source: Jim Manney, *God Finds Us: An Experience of the Spiritual Exercises of St. Ignatius of Loyola* (Chicago: Loyola Press, 2013), 77.

GOD

SO

LOVED....

<u>31</u>

THE BACKSLIDDEN

Billy Willis

Growing up I rarely went to church and didn't have a relationship with Jesus. That all began to change in 7th grade when my best friend, Chris, told me about a place that had free pizza. I was all in! I followed Chris as we rode our bikes, unsure of where we were going for this pizza, and as we approached our destination I realized it was a church. Inside, there was a youth group of about 15 other students and a few adults. One of those adults was Pastor Jack. At church that night, we played a game, sang songs, and Pastor Jack preached a short message. Afterwards, everyone hung out and some of us played basketball on a rickety old basketball hoop. It had all the elements of a typical youth group night, but you know what they didn't have? Pizza. I am still confused about that one!

I didn't get any pizza that night, but what I did get was an experience that ignited a relationship with Jesus. I had such a great time at youth group that it became a big part of my life each week. As summer camp approached, Pastor Jack offered me a scholarship to go and I went. I experienced home sickness right away. I was in a strange new place with a bunch of strangers. On the second or third night of camp, I encountered God for the first time in my life. After service I went to bed in tears, knowing Jesus was real. Later that week, I was baptized in the camp swimming pool. I returned home from camp that summer a new person.

The following school year, I was on fire for Jesus! I went to every youth group event there was. I wrote "Jesus saves" on my school notebooks, and invited kids at school to youth group. I was so hungry to grow closer to God and to learn about him that I bought a Children's Bible to read. I was 14 years old reading a book with more pictures than words! In addition to all that, I was so sold out for Jesus that if you told me something was a sin, I wanted nothing to do with it. I stopped lying, cheating, stealing, cussing, and lusting for girls. My close friends started to hide what they were doing from me—they were experimenting with drugs while I was experiencing a full life in Jesus Christ.

That all changed when I moved from Florida to Illinois. I became very lonely in this new place, and my desire for friendships slowly eclipsed my desire for Jesus. Eventually all the sins I had avoided before began to overtake me and sin crowded out my relationship with Him. I started drinking and getting high, and was open to experimenting with other drugs too. I also cussed, lied, cheated, stole, and lusted for girls now. I never denied Jesus with my mouth, but I denied Him by the way I lived my life. I was what's known as "backslidden." Being backslidden is when someone slides away from God and/or the church. If I had died at that time in my life, I'm not sure I would have gone to heaven.

While backslidden I still experienced conviction of sin, but I mistook the guilt I felt as condemnation. In John 16:8, Jesus explains that one of the jobs of the Holy Spirit is to convict us of sin. When we sin, we should feel guilty. The Holy Spirit uses guilt to convict us of sin and to draw us back to God. The devil, on the other hand, uses guilt to condemn and drive us further away from God. I believed the lie of the enemy, that my sin was too great for God to accept me, and I drifted further away from Him. I gave up on Jesus, but He never gave up on me. Romans 5:8 says, "God demonstrates His love for us in that while were still sinners, Christ died for us." When I wanted nothing to do with God, He still wants everything to do with me! So much so, that He strategically placed people in my path to be extensions of His love and truth in my life.

One of those people was a girl named Beth, a Christian I had some classes with. She had a sweet, loving personality and took a genuine interest in me. Many times we would talk about spiritual things. She knew I was a backslidden Christian and had a lot of confusion. Sometimes I would say ignorant things about God, but she never stopped caring about my relationship with Jesus and would tell me what the Bible actually said. She also invited me to her youth group and to a Christian club that met before school once a week. I began to feel closer to Jesus, but I didn't gain the traction I needed to fully surrender my life back to Him yet.

Another person God used was a friend and teammate named Jon. Jon and I first met in 8th grade, but he was a jock and I was not. We didn't begin a friendship until I joined the football team my sophomore year. Jon was a Christian, but he was far from a perfect. He was very plugged into his church and even played on the worship team, but he struggled with sin himself. He was pretty transparent about the temptations he faced, but he continued to live for Jesus. Like Beth, Jon would talk to me about his faith. He prayed for me and invited me to youth group. Most of the time I didn't go, but he never gave up. At the end of my junior year, after I fell the hardest into sin, Jon once again invited me to youth group. This time I went. That night became the catalyst to me coming back to Jesus once and for all.

That night I met Jeremy, Jon's new youth pastor. We connected and he took me under his wing to mentor me. Because of Pastor Jeremy's investment into my life, I grew closer than ever to Jesus that summer. I attended youth group every week, played board games at his house several nights a week, went to summer camp, and attended a Christian music festival with the youth group. By the end of summer I recommitted my life to Jesus and was on fire for Him again. All that I lost over the previous years was restored!

I am the product of a church kid's invitation to youth group. My story represents someone at your school who has fallen away from Jesus and is backslidden. Beth and Jon's role in my story represent the role God wants you to play in their life. I will never forget the part Beth, Jon, and Pastor Jeremy played in me coming back to Jesus. I am going to heaven because of their combined effort to reach out to the backslidden kid in their lives. God wants to use you in this way, and it's important to be persistent in strategic as you work to share Jesus with them.

Treat Them with Grace and Truth

How can you reach the backslidden student in your school? Do for them what Beth did for me. Love them and care for them despite their ugly flaws. Take a genuine interest in them as a person. Have spiritual conversations full of grace and truth (John 1:14). Be gracious when they say something untrue or ridiculous. Just listen, but then don't be afraid to tell them the truth either. Tell them the truth in love. Ask God to help you. Remember, "the Holy Spirit will teach you at that time what you should say." (Luke 12:12). Invite them to your Youth Alive Club or other Christian Club you attend.

Be Real With Them

Do for them what Jon did for me. Be real, be patient, and be persistent. Don't feel like you have to be perfect to display God's perfect love. Don't use God's grace as a license to sin, but show them that you can follow Jesus in the face of your struggle with temptation. Help them see that Jesus accepts people just the way they are and that He is the one who makes us a new creation in Christ (2 Corinthians 5:17). Pray with them and for them. Invite them to youth group and don't give up. Sometimes it takes many invitations before they finally agree to go.

Invest Yourself In Them

You may not be a youth leader, but you can do what Pastor Jeremy did for me by taking them under your wing and investing your time (and sometimes your money) into them. Make no mistake, making disciples (Matthew 28:19) will cost you something. Hang out with them. Drive them to youth group. Play boardgames with them. Go to a Christian concert together. Help them get to summer camp. Offer to help pay their way if you have to - whatever you can do, do it!

Having a Conversation

Someone is going to name you as a key person in their faith journey one day. There is nothing more rewarding than that. It starts now! It's as easy as asking a few questions that could ultimately lead them back to Jesus. Ask the question, lean in, and listen.

- **Tell me your story.** This a great way to show genuine interest in the person and get to know them. Ask follow up questions and recap parts of their story back to them to show that you are engaged. When they feel like you are interested in them, they will be more interested in what you have to say.
- **What role does faith play in your story?** If they haven't already brought up their faith yet, this is a great segue into spiritual things and it will help you know where they are coming from spiritually.

- **What does your relationship with Jesus look like right now?** Get to know where they currently stand with Jesus and identify if they've ever had a genuine relationship with Jesus or just a form of religion.

- **What does the Gospel mean to you?** Having a Biblical understanding of the Gospel is big deal. A misunderstanding of it can keep people from ever coming to faith in Jesus. Lovingly and graciously walk them through the Gospel using the *Alive In Five* resource or tools found in the back of this book. Do everything you can to help them understand the Gospel.

- **Do you feel like there is anything standing between you and Jesus?** Identify ways to pray for them and lovingly sharing the truth of God's Word with them.

- **Do you have any questions about Jesus or the Bible that I could help find answers to?** This will take some work on your end, but it will be worth it. You will personally grow from your research and you will help them see the authenticity of the Bible. There are a lot of great resources for finding Biblical answers to questions such as www.gotquestions.org.

GOD
SO
LOVED....

32
CULTURAL CHRISTIANS

Arin Nicholson

My friends and I grew up around church with some, like myself, attending every time the doors open and others dropping in for a week before and after camp, or joining us at fun conferences and retreats. Some of us were good academically but cussed like sailors in the locker room, while others jumped from relationship to relationship in between worship team practices. We were just normal students who liked to hang out, have fun, and not mess up too bad. The most common question we asked was some version of "how far was too far?" or "Is this a sin?" We didn't want to be too different that we stood out too much but also didn't want to be bad enough that God didn't love us anymore. We all had different ideas about how to live, but if you asked any of us the question, "What faith are you?" we would have responded with "Christian." I was a Christian by culture, but it hadn't really sunk into my heart. I wish I knew then how much more there was to falling in love with Jesus than simply trying to be a good person.

In the past there used to be an undertone amongst most American students that was felt but often unspoken. A common tie that without much attention held things together. That silent bond was church.

Church attendance and Christian ideals were commonplace and often fundamental to culture. That connection between faith and culture has shifted and Christian ideals are no longer most people's standard, but there is still a section of the population where growing up around faith or close to church has allowed them the opportunity to become what are known as "cultural Christians."

A cultural Christian is someone who identifies as a Christian but doesn't really live out a Christian life or exemplify the teachings of Jesus. They may identify as a Christian because their parents are Christian. They may have grown up going to church (regularly or not), or perhaps they just generally agree with what they believe Christianity is or what it represents. However, when you look at their life and actions, they may not really know what it means to be a follower of Jesus. Cultural Christianity is not rare, in fact in my own life I have been at times more a follower of Jesus by word than actual action, by culture more than conviction. It honestly would be a very good description of my friend group throughout high school. That all changed one day while eating chicken wings.

I was eating chicken wings on my birthday with my friends. My mom came around the corner and overheard us talking about how boring church was and joking about the girls we each were into. She asked me if the girl I liked was a Christian and I told her that I thought she was. My mom then looked at me as I bit into the next wing and said, "Well, is she helping other people know Jesus?"

I replied with, "Mom, I don't even do that much."

Then my mom hit me with the line, "Hmmm. So are you a 'church boy' or a Christian?" I don't think I ever finished the wing. I was really taken aback and challenged by what my mom had said. She was right. When it comes down do it, I'm not called to simply be a good person and carry a Christian title. I'm called to share Jesus. We all are.

At this point, a natural thing to consider is whether I am a cultural Christian or a genuine follower of Christ. What separates the two ideas? Although no one knows the state of someone's heart except for God, we do see that in John 13:35 it says, "By this everyone will know that you are my disciples, if you love one another."[1] The beauty of this verse is that it gives us one clear idea— that a person who genuinely follows

Jesus can be recognized by their love for other people. Love is something that is shared and something outside of ourselves. In many ways we can be confident in our relationship with God when it stops becoming about us, and our concern turns towards other people and our ability to help them grow in their faith as well.

This principle —that our relationship with God is not only about us but about loving and serving others—changed my life. It motivated me to have different conversations, to do more, to not settle for normal. Before I knew it, my friends saw the change in me and began to shift their lives as well. My life was changed because someone cared enough about me challenge my cultural Christianity, and my friends' lives were changed because I was able to challenge them in the same way.

Challenge

If you have friends who fit the definition of a cultural Christian and want them to be changed then I would encourage you to challenge them in the same way my mom challenged me. Cultural Christians have the benefit of sharing similar experiences and language. Many of them have been to church and/or agree with Christian values. You don't have to spend a lot of time explaining God, which allows you the opportunity to focus on the simple idea of living out what we say we believe in. John 13:35 reminds us that how we love defines our faith. Love is an action, and it isn't about you. Our faith becomes so much deeper and more layered when we begin to share it. I would go as far as saying there is no chance of your faith being only cultural when you are focused on sharing Jesus with others. Challenge your friends who are cultural Christians to join you in living a life defined by how you love others.

When you challenge your culturally Christian friends, keep your ratio in mind. Your ratio is a measure of how much you can challenge a friend without offending them. The stronger of a relationship you have, the more directly you can challenge them. My mom could call me out because we were close and I wasn't offended. Work hard at being a good friend with enough credibility in a person's life that you can ask hard questions or drop a nugget of truth and they will actually listen.

Talk about Jesus

If you want to reach cultural Christians with authentic, lived-out faith in Jesus, start by setting the example in your own life. If you're more than a cultural Christian, Jesus and the church should be showing up in your everyday conversations. Challenge yourself to talk about what

God is doing in your life with Cultural Christians, let your life be an example of God's reality. Take this point beyond every day normal conversations and set a goal to have intentional conversations with your culturally Christian friends about the state of the faith in Jesus. Make it more natural by inviting your friend to so something; go for ice cream and hang out at each other's houses. Even better, invite them to church. It's always more natural to have a conversation when you're doing things together.

You can really advance your intentional conversations by using prayer. You will be amazed at how the following phrase will change your life: "Can we pray about that?" The simple act of asking if you can pray with them is so powerful. Most people I have met are thankful that they are even asked.

Serve Together

Whether it's a Youth Alive campus club or something less official, an easy way for you to motivate and challenge a cultural Christian to be more than cultural is by loving others together. I have had the privilege of seeing tons of students use their creativity in various ways to spread the Gospel. From campus clubs focused encouraging faculty, to students using ultimate frisbee as an easy invite for kids on the fringes. Our faith excels when it's in action, and we excel when we do things together. So, create an outreach or serving project together. Find a group that needs help in your area and create a way to serve that group together.

Having a Conversation

Here are a few questions that will help you challenge and encourage cultural Christians to live an authentic life of faith. Remember, they should already be somewhat familiar with Jesus, so you can jump right into talking about God. Make your conversations count! Be honest about doubts and questions, and engage with them in healthy ways. Set aside time to talk about what you believe and push friends on their beliefs as well. What we talk about matters.

- **What is something God has spoken to you lately?** This question helps draw attention to the current state of their relationship with God. All of our lives should bear fruit and if theirs isn't then this is a good clarifying question.
- **Where do you go to church? What do you like most about it?** Many people who say they are Christians don't attend

church. So, bring it up and invite them to yours. This gives you a chance to reach out and help them find a strong community of support.

- **If you could help one group of people around here, what group would that be? What can we do to help them?** This is a great set of questions to ask if you want to create an outreach or serving project together. Remember, following Christ means loving others and telling them about Jesus. Taking action in response to the answers to these questions will help move your friend out of cultural Christianity and into the real deal.

- **What if we started something to share Jesus with our school?** Your friend's response might be, "Why would we do that?" This question creates the perfect opportunity to challenge cultural Christians, while also spurring the cultural Christian into action.

---

[1] NIV

GOD
SO
LOVED....

<u>33</u>

OTHER RELIGIONS

Lee Rogers

I met Bishal a few weeks ago while traveling in southeast Asia, and I enjoyed hearing his story over momos, a traditional Nepalese dish. Bishal was a committed Christ follower, and a leader in the church, but he did not grow up that way. In that part of the world there are many diverse religions with many diverse beliefs. It's not uncommon for each village, or region, to have its own religious system with different gods, goddesses, and practices. Bishal's family grew up believing there were many different gods, who represented many different things. There were good gods, who may grant you favor. There were also bad gods, who you had to appease with sacrifices in order to keep them from doing evil to you. Some good gods occasionally behaved badly, and some bad gods were known to occasionally behave generously. Just like the Greeks and the Romans, every god has it's own story in Bishal's religion.

He grew up in a house filled with idols, some of which represented gods, and some of which were believed to be gods themselves. As a teenager, Bishal began to express serious doubts over his family's religious practices. His parents were concerned, but Bishal was persistent. He could not believe there were so many different gods who behaved in so many different ways. He would pick up the idols in his house and throw them on the ground, demonstrating to his parents that they were not real because nothing happened to him as a result of his actions. "The gods did not punish me for throwing them to the floor, so this cannot be real!" Bishal declared to his parents.

Even though Bishal grew up in a remote village in a different part of the world, he was no stranger to education and science. Science was his real passion, and he went off to study it further at college. Soon he became ill, and had to return home. The illness became quite severe, and when he was close to death, his grandmother called the local witch doctor. The witch doctor came and offered sacrifices to the pagan gods, chanted rituals, and soon Bishal recovered. His perspective began to change again. He started to believe that some kind of power must exist, a power that we do not see, but that it couldn't all possibly be contained in the idols and traditions of his people, and it probably wasn't any kind of god at all. He believed it was an unknown, undiscovered, naturally occurring phenomenon. So he began his own investigation, attempting to uncover through scientific discovery and research, the source of healing power.

Bishal began traveling into remote forests and mountains that were said to contain evil gods, bringing with him scientific instruments to measure and capture whatever data he could on these unseen phenomena. Many times he attempted to document scientifically the supernatural forces everyone seemed to feel in these places, but he had no success. One trip, while returning from an investigation, he stopped to drink from a stream. His friends urged him not to drink the water, because the stream was thought to be possessed by powerful dark gods. Bishal did not believe gods were real, so of course he did not believe his friends when they told him the stream was possessed by dark gods. He drank from the stream, and that was the last thing he remembers.

Bishal woke up in his bed three days later with a witch doctor standing over him. He had passed out immediately after drinking the water, his friends had carried him back to his village, and the witch doctor had been performing rituals and sacrifices for the last three days, trying to revive him. His perspective began to change again. Although he still didn't believe in the idols, gods, and goddesses of his childhood, he started to believe supernatural powers and beings were real.

This time a new investigation began. Bishal started interviewing and having discussions with leaders from every religion he encountered; Hinduism, Buddhism, Islam, Confucianism, Kirantism, and even the local tribal religions. He wanted to collect as much knowledge, and as much teaching, as he possibly could, in order to figure out what these higher powers were. One day, while coming out of the mountains on a route he had never traveled before, Bishal came across a Christian missionary outpost. He and his friends stopped and asked for water, and the missionary began to share Jesus with them.

At first, Bishal listened because he was on an investigative journey of all religions in order to discover the truth. But soon he was drawn in by the Gospel story. As the missionary began to explain that there was only one God, who was light, and only one devil, who was darkness, everything began to make sense. Bishal had been partially correct all along—there were not many gods and idols that behaved erratically. But he had also been partially wrong—there really was a God, and there really was a devil. There was light, and there was darkness.

Bishal made several more trips to the missionary outpost, and had several more conversations with the missionary. It wasn't long before he surrendered his life to Jesus and made a full commitment to Christ, accepting the Gospel as true and placing his faith in God. Today Bishal is a leader in the church, and he teaches and mentors students who are studying the Bible to become pastors, missionaries, and leaders in many different countries.

It is estimated there are over 4,200 religions in the world today, each with a unique view of god, the afterlife, and the supernatural in general.[1] Here is something all those religions have in common: they believe something supernatural and powerful exists beyond what we see everyday. Most of them identify this as some kind of god or gods. In fact, 98% of the global population believes in a higher power.[2]

Scripture teaches the Holy Spirit is at work on a global scale, convicting the world of its sin, God's righteousness, and the coming judgment.[3] The Apostle Paul argued that man could recognize God's existence, even without any kind of religious instruction, just through the witness of nature and by man's own moral conscience.[4] All over the world, from the beginning of the human race until now, man has recognized a higher power exists through this work of the Spirit and the witnesses God provided, and they have tried to respond by creating their own religions.

Every religion is an attempt to respond to the witness the Holy Spirit has provided.[5] This is something we all have in common. But because of sin, those attempts to respond miss the mark. It is because of the blindness of sin that the world's religions fall short of recognizing God's love at it's fullest—in the sacrifice of Jesus Christ on the Cross, an act of love by a compassionate Savior for the redemption of all mankind.

While we have belief in a higher power in common with other religions, there are also many things that make Christianity unique and credible over the rest. The first unique truth is that our God is a holy God whose love is demonstrated in His own sacrifice. Our God doesn't sin, and he doesn't change. You won't find Him running around playing games like the Greek and the Roman gods did, and you'll never find him betraying His own nature by committing a sin. He is holy and perfect[6]; He always has been and He always will be.[7] He is perfect love, expressed through His own humble sacrifice.[8]

Every major religious system in the world requires that man work, or pay some kind of sacrifice, or obey some kind of code of laws in order to set things right with God. In Judaism, man must make a sacrifice and obey laws. In Islam, man must work for his salvation and obey the code of conduct. It's the same in every religion around the world: work and sacrifice, obey and work, sacrifice and obey and work. But this is not true with Christianity! This is the second unique thing about Christianity that makes it credible. In Christianity, man does not sacrifice or pay a price or work to earn his salvation. Instead, God is the one who makes the sacrifice, who pays the price, who does the work in order to earn man's salvation! This is the perfect love from a perfect God.

In Christianity, salvation is impossible to earn. It is grace that saves us, and that grace comes by faith in Jesus Christ.[9] This is a third distinct truth of Christianity that sets it apart from all the rest. Not only is salvation by grace through faith, it is also only available through Jesus Christ. This is the fourth unique truth of Christianity that sets it apart— Jesus is the only way to God.[10] No other religion makes this claim.

The apostle Paul recognized there were many different religions, and many different spirits at work in the world. That's why he wrote, "For although there may be so-called gods in heaven or on earth—as indeed there are many "gods" and many "lords"— yet for us there is one God, the Father, from whom are all things and for whom we exist, and one Lord, Jesus Christ, through whom are all things and through whom we exist."[11] He also wrote, "For we do not wrestle against flesh and blood, but against the rulers, against the authorities, against the cosmic powers over this present darkness, against the spiritual forces of evil in the heavenly places."[12] Make no mistake, there is only one God, but there are many dark spiritual forces of evil—the 'gods' and 'lords' that are recognized by the other religions—that are warring for the souls of mankind. We are a part of that battle, but our weapons are unique.

Engage in Conversation—A Lot

This book puts a lot of focus on having a conversation with the many different people groups in your school, but remember, most of those people groups are coming from a similar view of the world and religion as you. When it comes to reaching people from other religions with differing views of the world, it may require a lot more sincere conversations. In your conversations, you must take an interest in their perspective, their view of God, and their concept of salvation. You will not agree with them, but that is not as important, for the moment, as listening and learning. Before you can share your view, and point them to the God who's been calling out for them through the witness of the Holy Spirit, you've got to understand what they've believed. Through those conversations, you can probably affirm the thing they are getting right—belief in God—but also point them to the thing they've missed—Jesus Christ!

Invitations to Life and Fellowship

When you make a friend from another religion, see them as a friend first, and a member of another religion second. When you're friends first, you do the things that friends do together; you hang out, go over to each other's houses, and participate in the fun and pain of life together. When you've invited them into those normal parts of friendship, you're only one step away from inviting them into the fellowship of the church. If youth group and church are normal parts of your life, you should be inviting your friend to participate with you. And if they know church is important to you, it would actually be more awkward for you not to invite them. So keep the invitations rolling—first to full friendship, and then to fellowship with the Body of Christ.

Sacrifice in Love

If God's uniqueness is demonstrated through his sacrificial love, then we can demonstrate that our God is the only true God by also loving our friend in a sacrificial way. Please don't mistake me, I'm NOT asking you to die on a cross. But I am asking you to live according to Philippians 2:3-4, "Do nothing out of selfish ambition or vain conceit.

Rather, in humility value others above yourselves, not looking to your own interests but each of you to the interests of the others."[13] Demonstrating sacrificial love means going the extra mile for your friend—helping them with a project, buying them dinner, giving them a ride, encouraging them when they're sick. Even more than these things, it means considering their needs before your own. If you want to show that Jesus is the only way, demonstrate it by your love.

Having a Conversation

Understanding another person's religion, view of God, and concept of salvation can only be truly accomplished through a meaningful conversation. Here are some questions to get you started:

- **Tell me about your religion.** Okay, this is not a question, but it is a conversation starter. Let them tell you what they believe, and ask more questions whenever something peaks your curiosity. Listen and respect. You'll get a chance to share what you believe, also.

- **Do you have any special holidays or traditions that are part of your religious beliefs? What are your favorites? What makes those your favorites?** They almost certainly have an answer for this question, because religious holidays and traditions, in just about every culture, are as much about family as they are about religious belief. You won't just learn about the religious holidays, you'll learn about their family history. When you get your turn, be sure to talk about Christmas, but put the major emphasis on Easter. Easter is all about Jesus' victory over sin and death – it is the most important celebration in Christianity.

- **What do you think God is like? What do you believe about him?** Learning about the concept of God is important. You'll see how your views are different, and you'll also see the ways in which your views are similar. When it's your turn to talk about your ideas, make sure you talk about God's sacrificial love, and why it makes Him so unique.

- **What do you think about Jesus? Do you believe the things He said are true?** Remember, most major religions respect and honor Jesus in one way or another. If they express something like this, be sure to thank them, and then share your own beliefs about Jesus.

[1] http://www.adherents.com.

[2] http://www.religioustolerance.org/worldrel.htm.

[3] John 16:8.

[4] Romans 1:19-20, 2:14-16. Also Isaiah 6:3, "The whole earth is full of his glory."

[5] Andy Lord, "Principles for a Charismatic Approach to Other Faiths," in *Asian Journal of Pentecostal Studies*, 6:2 (2003), 239.

[6] Psalm 18:30, 1 Samuel 2:2, 1 Peter 1:15-16, Isaiah 6:3.

[7] Malachi 3:6, Hebrews 13:8.

[8] 1 John 4:8-10.

[9] Ephesians 2:8, Galatians 2:20.

[10] John 14:6.

[11] 1 Corinthians 8:5-6 ESV.

[12] Ephesians 6:12 ESV.

[13] NIV.

GOD SO LOVED....

34
HONORS STUDENTS

Chris Gillott

One month before I started my senior year of high school I left home to spend a month at Lynchburg University with a bunch of other rising seniors from all over the state of Virginia. The destination was Governor's School for Science and Technology. Few, if any, were star athletes or homecoming kings. Most of us were somewhat socially awkward and academically focused. Think about it—we had signed up to have additional homework during the summer. Of the thousands that had applied, a few hundred had been accepted. We had no idea what to expect, but we knew this would look good on a college application.

We jumped into our classes and quickly found our routines; we knew our way around a classroom! Some classes required quite a bit of study, and those students had to get acclimated to the University library. The rest of us had the evenings free, so we had to keep ourselves occupied. When we got tired of playing cards or Ultimate Frisbee, we ended up talking about anything and everything.

The conversation eventually turned to the topic of faith. I was certainly in the minority when I expressed my commitment to Christ. That wasn't a big deal, but I was shocked when another student basically made it his mission to hunt down any person of faith. He argued that we didn't know *why* we believed what we believed. He challenged any Christian saying, "You just believe what your parents believe."

I grew up in church attending an endless number of services and special events. I had responded to countless altar calls and had helped lead many ministry activities. But in many ways, this moment when I was away from home and the security of my Christian community, was the moment where I felt my faith became my own.

✳ ✳ ✳

Many academic environments are increasingly hostile to faith. Many students feel the weight of the implicit analogy "intellectual is to atheist as ignorant is to religious." Popular figures like Richard Dawkins, Sam Harris, Stephen Hawking, and even Bill Maher go a step further and preach that the world would be a better place without any people of faith. This attitude may be popular with some, but it is not well founded.

Throughout history and still today, people of faith are among the people most likely to be found doing good. They serve the marginalized and the needy. They give to charity at a remarkable rate. All around this country and all around the world communities have flourished where Christians have arrived and built hospitals and universities. Some of the best known Universities have Christian roots; among them are Harvard, Yale, Princeton, Dartmouth, Columbia, William and Mary, Rutgers, and Brown. In fact, with very few exceptions, all of the first universities founded in America were founded to promote the Christian faith. Many of the scientists who led the enlightenment pursued their science out of devotion to God.

Even today, huge numbers of Christians have earned respect in academic circles. Here are a few along with their accomplishments:

- John Lennox, renowned author and mathematician who studied at both Oxford and Cambridge
- Francis Collins, former Director of the Human Genome Project and director of the National Institutes of Health
- Ian Hutchinson, Professor of Nuclear Science at MIT
- Ben Carson, Director of Pediatric Neurosurgery at Johns Hopkins Hospital and the first surgeon to successfully separate conjoined twins
- One of the highest ranking leaders in The Assemblies of God, Jim Bradford, holds a Ph.D. in aerospace engineering.

Becoming a Christian has never required you to turn off your brain, so don't believe the myth.

One of the big obstacles to sharing Jesus with many students is that they've heard the Bible cannot be trusted. It's important that we don't expect that they will believe the Bible at face value, or the conversation will be over before it starts. Instead, as a relationship begins to grow, they will eventually learn that they can trust you and trust the Bible.

> *Then the eleven disciples went to Galilee, to the mountain where Jesus had told them to go. When they saw him, they worshiped him; but some doubted.*
> Matthew 28:16-17 NIV

One of the unique beauties of the Christian faith is that it invites us to come with our questions and doubts. We don't have to pretend all of it makes sense to us. God welcomes our doubts, questions, and confusion. Doubt isn't toxic to faith.

> *He answered, "'Love the Lord your God with all your heart and with all your soul and with all your strength and with all your mind'; and, 'Love your neighbor as yourself.'"*
> Luke 10:27 NIV

This is a clear reminder that loving God is not a mindless act; it involves every part of you. That love also shapes and inspires the love you have for others.

> *But in your hearts revere Christ as Lord. Always be prepared to give an answer to everyone who asks you to give the reason for the hope that you have. But do this with gentleness and respect,*
> 1 Peter 3:15 NIV

This is part of your challenge. It reminds you to share the truth and explains how you should share it.

Most honors students are not looking for another activity or extra-curricular; they've already chosen the ones they think will look best on scholarship and college applications. They are not looking for a reason to be out late on a school night. They are certainly not looking for a reason to get up early on Sunday morning. But please, do invite them to your Bible Club and your church services. Most people like to be invited to things because it makes them feel valued.

Connecting Them To Service Project Ideas

Some honors students have to find ways to fulfill community service requirements. If you have the same assignment, you have inside information. Your church or youth ministry might be able to connect them to an organization or family that needs help. It's a chance to do something your church supports and help them fulfill a requirement, all while inviting them to interact with the community of faith.

Be a Great Classmate

For many of these students, academics is the number one priority in life. If you affect their grades for better or worse, your influence will be directly affected. Do what you can to make sure the classes you share go as well as possible. If you're assigned a group project or presentation, make sure you do your part within the timeline the group sets. When you're together, make sure the group stays on task. This might seem like something a school teacher would say, but if the person you're trying to reach is most focused on their grades, this will earn you their respect and a listening ear.

Throw A Study Party

If there's a major test or exam, find a place and time to study together. This might happen at your house, or a teacher might even agree to stay in their classroom over lunch and allow you to meet there. Make sure the people that come are really coming to study. Come up with a plan to get some food so you can snack while you work. Prepare study supplies like flash cards or study sheets from test summaries. Having everything prepared and in place will make your time more productive AND more fun (and may lead to another study party).

Having a Conversation

Many achieving students are very comfortable with challenging conversations, but disagreement is not the best place to start. Also, they might be on the debate team, so you might be setting yourself up for disaster. Instead, try to build a genuine connection before you ever push a hot-button. Also, don't pretend to answer a question you don't know, because it will make you look *intellectually* dishonest, not to mention *simply* dishonest.

Here are some questions to help you get a conversation rolling:

- **What do you hope to do after High School? Where do you plan to go? What do you plan to study? What will you do with your degree?** This is a question they've probably thought about quite a bit—and they most likely have a detailed plan. Get to know them better by listening well to what they hope to do. Plus, everyone likes it when someone takes an interest in them.

- **What subject are you enjoying the most this semester?** Achieving students love to succeed. They will enjoy talking about what is going well. This can offer you an opportunity to express admiration or encouragement.

- **If you could choose any of the awards the school gives out at the end of the year, which ones would you pick and why?** This question will show what they value and what they want to achieve in the long run. It will also allow you to shift towards the bigger picture of what you hope your life will achieve.

- **What do you think happens after a person dies?** This is a hugely significant question for obvious reasons. But not only does it point to spiritual truth, it also highlights a question that science cannot answer.

- **What do you believe about the origins of the universe? Was it created through random circumstances, or is there a possibility of a creator?** Almost every scientist today believes the universe had a beginning, a point of origin. This idea is as old as the Genesis story, but it was popularized in science by Georges Lemaître, a Belgian priest and astronomer who proposed the theory of the expansion of the universe. Today it's popularly known as "The Big Bang Theory." Ultimately, this is a question about the existence of a Creator. Do some research on "Intelligent Design Theory," and you'll find there's a lot of good scientific thought in this direction. But ultimately, belief in a Creator is about faith in what we cannot see or prove. This is where your testimony has to come in. You should talk about the science of it all, but remember to share your experience of belief as well.

GOD SO LOVED....

35

STUDENT LEADERS

Wes Sheley

Not long ago, I sat down with a principal in western Oregon to discuss how we could help his school with the difficulties they'd been through. Within six months they had a student commit suicide, another one killed in an accident, and two teachers had been arrested in different situations. As a Youth Alive Missionary, I wanted to do anything I could to serve the Principal and his school campus. The Principal was searching for anything to help his school through this season, so we set a meeting. The meeting was supposed to last only ten minutes, but turned into an hour and a half listening to the Principal's heart for his school, especially his students.

We began to discuss putting together a school assembly called The 7 Project. I've done The Seven Project many times throughout Oregon, but felt a special emphasis on this one due to the circumstances. One thing the Principal repeated over and over again was, "Let me check with the Student Leadership class." Nothing was going to happen unless the student leaders of the school were behind it.

A few days later we sat down with the student leaders and I could tell they were skeptical about another assembly program coming to their school. It turns out we were going to be the third assembly within three months. We began to layout the school assembly to the leadership class and shared that we use local people to be the speakers and that they get to pick the topics. Through the discussion, we learned that as a class they wanted to have more of an impact in local elementary schools. Hearing this, we offered to put together an assembly program with them, so they could present and be the speakers for the elementary schools. They overwhelmingly voted "YES."

We began a three-year journey, not just with the Principal, but also with the student leadership class. In those three years we presented The 7 Project to the high school twice, and they formed their own elementary school assembly, presenting it to schools in their community. The most important thing we were able to do was to connect our local speakers, youth pastors, directly with the leadership class. Seeing youth pastors connect to the student leaders of the school, working together to craft assemblies oriented around community transformation, was a powerful moment. The best part of it all was seeing the youth pastors walk into the class and seeing students from their youth group in the class.

Every school has a student leadership class. Sometimes it's called "Student Council" or "Student Government," but nearly every high school has some type of leadership organization or system for students. Whatever it's called, this group is one of the most powerful and influential groups in the school today. This group has direct influence on the school calendar and what goes on it, the culture and direction of the school year, and the atmosphere of the school campus. Imagine what would happen if the student leadership group was full of Christ-believing students guiding and directing our campuses, and having a voice to school administration. What would happen if Christ-believing student leaders could invite their youth pastors or leaders to get involved in what the school was doing?

There is a shift happening within school administrations all across the country; they are making decisions in different ways than they have in the past. This shift may be the key to how you can reach your school and help change the atmosphere on your campus. More and more, principals consult with student leaders before making decisions that affect student culture.

I've heard it said, "In order to change the culture you need to be in the culture." If you want to see your school changed, you need to be involved in a meaningful way. I watched the Christ-believing students in that leadership class start taking important roles on their school campus.

It was these students that had a purpose/cause in everything that they did for their school. By placing themselves in a situation to steer the culture around them, they set an example to others that there is purpose in life, and they ultimately steered their friends towards Christ.

These students, much like you, had an ultimate goal to see their friends and their school know Jesus. They weren't standing on cafeteria tables telling the school to repent, but they *were* inviting students to community service projects, fundraising for good causes, and inviting outside groups to influence the culture on the campus. Their role on the campus created personal conversations with others that allowed them to share their testimony of what Jesus has done in their lives.

Fully Commit

"Commit your way to the Lord; trust in him and he will do this: He will make your righteousness shine like the dawn, the justice of your cause like the noonday sun."
Psalm 37:5-6 NIV

What a great verse for student leaders! The best way we can lead others is by our commitment, and there is no commitment greater than the one we make to the Lord. If you are in the student leadership group at your school, or even at your church, this verse should speak loudly to you. Everything you do in these groups has a purpose. When we commit our ways to the Lord, He will provide opportunities for our faith to shine and for your Jesus story to be heard.

Fully Serve

"For even the Son of Man did not come to be served, but to serve, and to give his life as a ransom for many."
Mark 10:45 NIV

One of the greatest reflections of Jesus through your life in today's culture is to serve others. Approach your student leadership group with this first thought, "How can I serve you?" I have learned that when I approach people with this attitude they are caught off guard. That's because it's not a common attitude in today's culture, which tells me that it is a part of Christ that is missing in today's culture. Jesus came to serve, not be served. What would happen if you showed up to school tomorrow with the thought, "How can I serve my school today? How can I serve my friends today? How can I serve Jesus today?" If you do this, I guarantee that your day tomorrow will not look like it did today.

Be Humble

"Do nothing out of selfish ambition or vain conceit,
but in humility consider others better than yourselves."
Philippians 2:3 NIV

This is one of the hardest things to do as a natural leader, besides being a servant. It's in our nature to want people to notice our accomplishments. One habit great leaders practice is to put others before themselves, and to acknowledge others before themselves. If you do this, you will find your fellow student leaders will be more likely to listen to you, and even follow where you are leading. They will trust you more. They will listen to what you say, especially when you are able to share how Jesus makes the difference in your life. It all starts with humility.

Pray

Pray for your School, your student leadership organization, and the principal. Pray for ways and areas to serve in. Everything starts with prayer. Before I approached that high school in Oregon, I spent a lot of time in prayer. I found the more I prayed for the school, the more my heart broke for the school. I found I was becoming more and more in tune to what God wanted to do on the school campus, and how He wanted it to be done.

Having a Conversation

Here are some questions to help you have great conversations with your fellow student leaders. Some of these will help you have a personal conversation that leads to Jesus, while others will help you connect with some of the broader things God may be wanting to do in your school.

- **What draws you to be a leader? What do you find most fulfilling about it?** Listen to what your friend has to say. Be prepared to share your own perspectives on leadership, and especially how your relationship with Jesus impacts this.
- **Have you ever felt like you were born to be a leader? What does that say about how each person is designed?** This is a conversation about how God gifts each person with uniqueness. Not everyone is a leader, and according to Romans 12:8, it's a gift God gives to certain people. Be prepared to share your perspective on this. You can even share the verse, because it will help start a conversation about God and the Scriptures.

- **Jesus was arguably the most influential leader in history. What did He say about leadership? In what ways did his life match that message?** Be prepared to share Jesus' lesson on leadership from Mark 10:43-45. Leadership is accomplished through serving. Jesus became a servant to all through the Cross. This is a great way to share the message of the Gospel.

- **What are the biggest challenges facing our student body? What can we, as a leadership group, do to help this situation?** This is a great question to assess the needs of your school, and to discover how God may want to work through you and your fellow leaders to address those needs.

- **What are some of the things we can do to serve our school? What groups from outside of the school could help us?** If leadership for a Christian is ultimately about serving, help your student leadership group to start moving in this direction. When you talk of bringing in groups from outside to help, be sure to mention your church, or other area churches as a resource. They would probably jump at the opportunity to be involved in the local school.

GOD

SO

LOVED....

<u>36</u>

TEACHERS

Christine Rogers

Sixth graders are awesome. I mean seriously—falling in love for the first time, hugging friends who are having a bad day, farting in the middle of class, running in the hall to get to their next class (even if they don't like that class), questioning everything, matching every outfit with florescent anything, can't dance but love going to dances— AWESOME! What's even better is that lots of you reading this are older than sixth graders and you just thought...that's still me! If that's the case, I think you're pretty awesome too!

Every year I teach 100 of the silliest, smelliest, funniest, most compassionate, and incredibly talented sixth graders on the planet. Not too long ago, Ami was in my class. She was tall for an eleven-year-old, with dark brown eyes and an easy smile. She wasn't a leader, but wasn't a follower either. She just did her own thing and the other kids watched. Not the 'staring at her' kind-of-watched, more like the 'Hmmm, that's interesting, I'll see how it goes for her' kind-of-watched. For some genuinely sad reasons, her parents weren't around and she lived with her grandma. Grandma was awesome; I wish I had her as a sixth grader.

Having no parents can leave a pretty big hole in a kid, and grandma did everything she could to help to fill it, including introducing Ami to Jesus. I don't know all the 'whens' or 'hows'—I just know that when Ami entered my sixth-grade science class, she loved Jesus and wanted to share it with everyone...even her teachers.

And I'm going to pause right here because I'm a part of this story.

Not a big part, but I thought you might like to know how I felt as a teacher when a student wanted to share Jesus with me: I felt loved...like all warm-and-gooey loved. You might be thinking, "Well if you didn't believe what she believed, you would have been irritated." Nope. I've had students of other beliefs share with me too. I've always felt loved. I acknowledge that if a student believes that everyone should know about his or her belief, I feel honored to be included.

For what it's worth, I happen to know a lot of my students are Christians and they never tell me about Jesus. And I kind of wonder why they don't think I'm important enough to hear about Jesus. Sure, you and I know that I already know about Jesus, but they don't know that.

So anyway, back to the story.

During her study hall period, Ami would write a blog about Jesus. It was just a short blog about her weekend and how God had helped her in some way. It always had a bible verse at the end. Sometimes it was funny. Sometimes it didn't make much sense. It always had really bad spelling and it was always awesome. She asked me if I would follow her blog, so I did. Pretty soon other kids were following her blog, too. She asked other teachers to follow her blog and they all did, too. That's because teachers really like students; we want to be a part of your life.

But then...THEN...

Remember that hole that Ami had in her life—no parents and all? She got angry one day. Actually, she got angry a lot of days but had learned how to stop and pray for peace. But one day, she got angry and didn't stop to pray for peace. Instead, she stopped and punched a kid in the nose. KA-POW!

And nothing spreads faster in middle school then news of a fight. Now, Ami was 'that kid who had punched someone'.

I was talking with some teachers who had been following Ami's blog, and one of them mentioned the fight. I should point out that none of the teachers were sixth-grade teachers, so they didn't know Ami's history. One of the teachers wasn't a Christian. This was a teacher that I had been praying for and talking about Jesus with for over four years.

The teacher looked at me and said, "No offense," (you know something offensive is about to come anytime someone says, 'no offense'), "but I knew this would happen. This always happens with Christians. They say one thing about love and then do something totally different."

Cue me shriveling up and dying just a bit inside. Ok, maybe a lot. Four years. FOUR YEARS. Four years I had been praying for this teacher.

Months passed, classes were taught, lunches were eaten, and snow days came and went. I began to repair some of the damage done to this teacher's budding faith by talking with her about what Christianity looked like, and how it didn't look like perfection. And in case you were wondering, I still thought Ami was awesome.

Lucky for me, I wasn't working on repairing the damage alone. Of course, the Holy Spirit was working (props!), but so was Ami. Remember that awesome grandma I mentioned? She talked to Ami about how that fight changed how others looked at her as a Christian. And so, she started making things right. She apologized to the kid she punched. She apologized on her blog. She apologized to kids in person. And she walked around and apologized to every teacher that had read her blog.

I came back from lunch to find a hand written note slipped onto my desk:

Dear Mrs. Rogers,

Im sory that I punched Kim. I was mad but that's no icsuse. Just rember that Jesus didn't punch Kim. Jesus loves everyone even you.

Sincerly,

Ami (your favrite science kid)

All warm and gooey. That's how I felt.

Remember that teacher I had been praying for? After Ami talked with her, she was really quiet about Christianity for a few months. She just said, "Ami apologized to me today. How crazy is that? I've never had that happen before. It was really amazing."

In her life, that was all it took to repair the damage. Towards the end of the year, she began bringing up some of the verses that Ami was sharing on her blog and we began to move forward again.

HEY!!! Did you catch that?!? The teacher was bringing up verses that she was reading off of Ami's blog!!!

"Do your best to present yourself to God as one approved, a worker who does not need to be ashamed and who correctly handles the word of truth."
2 Timothy 2:15 NIV

So let's be honest. If you are presenting yourself to God in this way, you are also presenting yourself to others in this way. It doesn't mean you are perfect. No one is perfect. Look at the beginning of that verse again. "Do your best…" That's what God wants from all of us. And that's really what your teachers want from you. And when you mess up, when you are ashamed because you haven't handled the word of truth with integrity, you need to work long and hard to make it right. Apologize. That's what God wants from us, too. And that's what could really affect your teachers outlook.

Ideas for Connecting with Teachers

- **Do what you say.** If you are talking about Jesus, make sure your actions match your words. Your actions are noticed. I notice when a student stops in the hallway to help someone pick up dropped belongings. I notice when someone works in a group with an "annoying" student without demeaning that student. I notice when a student works hard even when they don't feel like it. I notice when a student sticks up for something that is right even if his friends don't. I notice when a student tells the truth even if it gets her into trouble. It's all about integrity.

- **Food.** Let me repeat that—Foooooooooooood. Teachers love food. A tray of brownies placed in the teachers' lounge with a note saying, "Thank you for all you do as a teacher and God bless," goes a long way. Seriously. Food.

- **If there is a specific teacher that God has placed on your heart, write them a note and say just that.** Something like, "I believe in God. I believe that I can talk to God and he talks to me. He has put you on my heart so I'm praying for you." I'm sure you're a much better writer, but you get the idea.

- **If you ever get to choose a topic to do a project on, choose one about God or your testimony.** Always. This is the easiest way to "talk" to a teacher. But you have to rock that project! Think about if you worked in a pizza shop and were making a pizza with the word Jesus spelled out in pepperoni to give to the pizza shop owner. If you hand the pizza shop owner a broken pizza that had been dropped on the floor and you had forgotten to add the cheese but had spelled out the word Jesus beautifully, the owner is going to associate Jesus with gross pizza and sloppy work. Same with the teacher. Make an awesome pizza so we can appreciate the Jesus in it.

Having a Conversation

To this day, I'm sure Ami has no idea about her part in my teacher-friend's walk towards the Lord. And that's because this conversation is different from many of the other conversations that you are reading about in this book. A student's conversation with a teacher is one sided. The student talks and the teacher listens.

It's weird, I know. But here's why it's one sided. You're under 18, and we are in a professional relationship (teacher and student). The topic you are having a conversation with us about is personal (faith). It's personal for you and personal for us. It's okay for teachers to share some personal information—my students know who my husband is, see pictures of my son, and know all about how I like to backpack on the Appalachian Trail. But it's not usually okay for teachers to share bigger personal things with students during school hours. It's unprofessional, and it could get them into big trouble if it's perceived the wrong way. Religious beliefs count as a bigger personal thing. Sometimes, especially during school hours, a teacher could even be seen as breaking the law by talking about God.

But that doesn't mean YOU can't talk about God. In fact, *you're the only one in school who can freely talk about God.* So keep talking even if you think no teacher is listening! Keep acting with integrity, even if you think no teacher is watching. Keep writing, even if you think teachers don't care. Keep apologizing, even if you don't think you'll be forgiven.

We are listening and watching and caring and forgiving. And we'd like to know that you think we are worth sharing Jesus with.

GOD
SO
LOVED....

<u>37</u>

VO-TECH STUDENTS

Kami Kirschbaum

This time last year I was praying to God and asking if He wanted me to apply for a Vocational-Technical career opportunity at my high school. At this point in my life, I was an active Campus Missionary—a student committed to sharing Jesus at school. I was familiar with how to reach out to my high school. It didn't happen everyday, but I felt comfortable talking about uncomfortable things with my peers, and God did break my heart for them over and over again. I prayed, "God, please only let me go to Vo-Tech if you have people there who desperately need you." And at the end of my freshman year in high school, I applied for cosmetology at my Vo-Tech school and was accepted. I was really excited for a new season of my life, but I was also kind of intimidated by having to find my way in a brand new mission field.

My prayers were answered the second day of school in a Vo-Tech gym class. I approached a shy redhead in the corner and asked her what her name was. Ashley began opening up and started telling me about what music she likes, how she ended up at my Vo-Tech, and even what she believed and why! God totally opened this door, and I was overwhelmed with opportunity when she started pouring her heart out to me.

We had completely different views; I loved God and had a solid relationship with Him, and she was agnostic. But Ashley was exploring many different things. Through daily conversations, and getting to know her better, I really gained respect for her. She also let me share my heart, and even started attending church services with me. The Gospel was

239

presented to her because someone was willing to give her the time of day, accept her, and actively listen to her.

If you are not a Vo-Tech student, I want to let you in on our world a little bit, particularly what it feels like to study for a trade. Vo-Tech students are often looked down upon because we tend to not be high achievers in academic subjects like math and science. We are high achievers in other areas of life and study, but not always at those academic subjects.

It doesn't just feel like non-Vo-Tech students look down upon us, it also feels like the entire educational system considers us a bit less than the rest. We are sent to a different school for part of the day, we don't get recognized in many of the awards assemblies and banquets, and increasingly schools are placing the majority of their focus on getting students into college, leaving us behind in matters of funding and attention. We Vo-Tech students are among 'the least of these' in today's educational system.

The truth about intelligence is that it comes in many different varieties. In fact, a Harvard professor developed a widely accepted theory that there are eight different types of intelligence, and the traditional academics only fit into two of the eight kinds.[1] That means we Vo-Tech students possess high intelligence in areas other students do not, even though we are not recognized for our uniqueness and achievement. There are brilliant doctors and lawyers who don't know the first thing about changing oil in a car, or using hand tools, let alone the more intricate craftsmanship and skills that Vo-Tech brings out in us. So remember, even if you've considered us among the 'least of these' in the past, we have significant intelligence, and we have a significant contribution to make to society.

The Bible teaches us to accept one another just as Christ accepted us. This is not an easy concept for everyone, however the Apostle Paul writes, "Accept one another, then, just as Christ accepted you, in order to bring praise to God."[2] This verse is teaching us that one of the ways we worship God is through how we treat people! Accepting people creates room for God to work in your conversations. Accepting the 'least of these' is God's work through us.

If God has given us a broken heart for the lost and the 'least of these', then we need to pray, "How can we reach these students?" A lot of them put up all kinds of walls towards letting people in, have doubts about trusting others, and are skeptical of religion. I've found the most effective way to connect is simply through friendship. If you are genuinely interested in a person, that will make them notice something really different about you. You'll find that as your kindness and caring heart grows, you will begin to understand and connect with people in more effective ways.

Friendship that Matters

In order to share Jesus with a Vo-Tech student, you have to create a friendship that matters. That means loving and appreciating them for who they are; taking time to hear their stories, and spending time together outside the classroom. Once a meaningful friendship is developed, it is a blessing to watch it grow. It doesn't always happen instantaneously, you've got to work at it. As your meaningful relationships begin to develop, find ways to connect these relationships to God and the church. One idea is to have a get-together night with devotionals that are centered on your trade. For example, I'm a cosmetology student, and I could host a girls' night at my house. I would invite a youth leader, or my youth pastor, to drop in and share an encouraging devotional they can apply to their trade. Alternatively, I could create and present the devotional myself.

Serve Your Peers

There are many different ways to serve, but serving in a way that opens up doors to share Jesus requires intentional thought and planning. One idea is to ask the school administration about giving everyone a snack with an encouraging message on it. It's a sacrifice, but it's a very practical way to show some Christ-like love to your fellow students. It can really change the way people see you, especially if you're a Christian. Plus, who doesn't love rice crispy treats that look like pumpkins or hearts or Christmas trees?! If doing something like this on a school-wide scale is intimidating, just start with your class. Finding creative ways to serve creative people is not only effective, it's also a part of exploring who God made you to be.

Connect Craftsmanship to God's Work

Trades keep the world going; they are the everyday expression of service to our community. Our boys in carpentry literally build houses with their hands, tools, and materials. This is craftsmanship, and the

Word of God says a lot about it! In fact, God often portrays Himself as a craftsman. In Job 28, He asks the questions:

> "Where were you when I laid the foundation of the earth? Tell me, if you have understanding. Who determined its measurements—surely you know! Or who stretched the line upon it? On what were its bases sunk, or who laid its cornerstone, when the morning stars sang together and all the sons of God shouted for joy?" [3]

God is using the words and describing techniques of the carpentry trade—foundation, measurements, sinking the bases, laying a cornerstone, stretching a line—these are terms and techniques we still use today in construction. God is a craftsman, and craftsmanship is God's work.

In auto-mechanics they're learning how to build an engine, and a lot of other things that I will never understand about cars. These are practical things that an elective in a traditional high school won't teach you. These trades set us apart. For me, in cosmetology, we have days where clients can come in and we get to serve them and practice our skills. In your tech, sooner or later, you'll have a chance to interact with someone who needs something created or fixed. If you offer yourself, outside of the school walls, God will use that! And your classmates are going to see that, and wonder why you're going above and beyond. This is a great conversation starter, and I've found that my peers usually want to serve right next to me. If you choose to let God use you in this field, it will bring up great conversations that can lead to Jesus.

Having a Conversation

Once you have a solid relationship with students that you can relate to easily, you need to start investing in these friendships by asking them thought-provoking questions. Asking questions that matter, that make students think about purpose, will ultimately point them to the Lord. The reality is that most teens *do* think about these things, but sometimes they are not bold enough to talk about it. When you begin to venture into a person's life by asking purposeful questions, you will eventually reap what you sow. Purpose-driven questions lead to purpose-driven relationships. Some questions that you could ask friends, or potential friends, that would point to God would be:

- **What made you interested in this field?** Proverbs 20:5 says, "The purposes of a person's heart are deep waters, but one who has insight draws them out." [4] Once you begin asking your friend what 'purposed' them to do what they do, it will make them think and it will help you understand them. This question points to God's creation, passion, and drive inside of us to discover our purpose.

- **In a perfect world, what will you do with this trade in five years?** This question is so open and has so much potential! No matter what trade you're in, the sky is the limit. Find out where they see their life headed, and if God is part of their thinking. Be ready to share your own vision. When God is incorporated into your dreams, your potential stretches beyond the sky—it's limitless.

- **What is your purpose in this trade?** This is a very broad question you should ask because it shows there can be a chance of purpose in a trade, the future, and even life. Even if they blow you off, this is still a question they're going to have to think about.

- **In what ways does your trade make a difference?** I think this question can open up a whole new part of your friend's mind— showing him or her you think they do have potential. Letting them know someone believes in them will go beyond what you'll ever see.

- **Where does creativity come from?** This question matters because it is extremely open ended. This will give you a really good idea of where their head is at with creation itself, and where creativity is born. Ultimately it can point to God. This question will open up opportunities for God to do something great.

---

1 http://www.cse.emory.edu/sciencenet/mismeasure/genius/research02.html.
2 Romans 15:7 NIV.
3 Job 38:4-7 ESV.
4 NIV.

PART III

CONCLUSION

38

LOOKING FORWARD

Lee Rogers

Something funny happened when I went to college. I attended the University of Valley Forge in southeastern Pennsylvania, a small but excellent Christian college with a Pentecostal spirituality. I went to this college to study for ministry, and many of the friends I made there also attended for the same reasons. I expected college to be different from high school, and it definitely was. The university president used to say, "College is for character, not just for education."[1] That character was tested and reformed as each of us experienced the world apart from our parents and the strict structure of the public school system for the first time in our lives.

But in another sense, college was no different from high school. I discovered the same groups of people that were in my high school also existed in my college; the academic students, artists, and athletes were all there. There were quiet students and nerds, student leaders and outdoorsmen. The underprivileged were there, and so were the hurting. Every different people group I encountered in high school, I also found waiting for me in college. This is a lesson in life—you will encounter the same types of people almost everywhere you go. Looking forward, whether you join the workforce, enter a technical school, join the army, or go to college, the same groups of people will be there waiting for you. But that doesn't mean life will be the same.

College was different, even though the people were the same. The difference was me. I was more open to friendships with all kinds of people, no matter what group they would normally fit into. I was ready to leave the stereotypes and limitations of the past behind. I was ready for a fresh start. I was willing to be friends with anyone, because everyone is created in God's image. I only wish I'd come to this point of realization and clarity sooner.

If you can make friends and share Jesus with many different people from many different groups *now*, you will be so far ahead in sharing Jesus *later*. God so loved *the world*. This is the most inclusive statement of God's love in Scripture. No one is exempt from the love of God. Looking forward, God is calling you to share Jesus wherever you go, with whomever you meet. And if you are open to the Spirit's leading, you will meet all kinds of different people.

I grew up in rural Pennsylvania, attended a small high school, and was into the arts. I'm white, grew up in a middle class home, and started driving my first car at 16 years of age. I thought that God would place me in ministry among people just like me, because I thought that was where I would be the most effective. It's not the first time I've been wrong about what God was going to do, and it probably won't be the last.

The first summer of my college experience, I was serving at a youth camp as a chaperone. I was assigned to a group of students by the camp, responsible to provide them with supervision and leadership for the entire week. I have to admit that when I met them I was intimidated, because they were nothing like me. They were all African American and came from the inner city. I didn't know how this was going to work out. The first day was pretty rough. I struggled to gain their cooperation, and I even had to be firm with them a couple of times. I wanted to help them find Jesus, to sense God's love touching their hearts, and to see them have an experience with the Holy Spirit. But now I didn't know how we would make it through the week.

I prayed, "God, how can I lead people who are so different from me?"

God responded, "In the same way that I died for them; in love."

By the end of the next day we were praying together at the altars, having fun together during free time, and struggling alongside each other in the team competitions. I got to know them, and they found me to be genuinely interested in them and concerned for them. At the end of the week we said goodbye as brothers, not as strangers from different groups. I didn't know that God would call me to be a youth pastor in Philadelphia just one year later. I ended up leading a youth group full of city kids, and some of them with some very dark backgrounds. They were so different from me, but God so loved them. I stayed in that city church for almost five years, until God called me back to the rural setting I grew up in. I am friends with many of those students to this day, though they aren't students anymore.

God so loved *the world*. God so loved everyone who is different from you. I've shared a cup of cocoa and Christ with a Tanzanian named Noah on the slopes of Mount Kilimanjaro in Africa. After a week in a tent together, I've laughed, cried, and prayed at the altar with Yupik Eskimo teenagers on the Yukon River Delta, as God reached through their brokenness and restored their joy. I've stepped out and bought dinner for a new friend, Samuel, and we felt the Spirit knit our purposes together; one year later I spent three weeks with him in his home in India, sharing Jesus and training future leaders to impact youth for the Gospel. I had nothing in common with any of these people, except for God's love and conversation. Through our conversation, the Holy Spirit built a bridge between us, and the Gospel was realized. God so loved *the world*, and so should we.

Looking forward, you cannot predict where God will take you, or how your life will end up, or whom you will spend it with. You can plan, but you cannot predict. One thing you can say for certain is, wherever you go, whomever you meet, and however you spend your time, God so loved *the world*. So get to know people who are different from you *now*. Use the chapters in this book to start conversations with those who have different interests from you, who grew up in different life situations, and who believe different things. Serve everyone around you. Share the Gospel without prejudice, recognizing that the Gospel is for *everyone*. God so loved *the world*, and that begins with the realization that God so loved *your school*.

---

[1] Dr. Don Meyer, President of the University of Valley Forge.

APPENDIX
SHARING JESUS AS A HOMESCHOOLER

Aaron Benick

It was Youth Convention 2013 and my buddy, Lee Rogers, had asked me if I wanted to help him out during the weekend. I excitedly accepted. Like most teenagers usually do, I met a lot of interesting people that weekend, and one interesting girl in particular. She was pretty cute, and seemed like the kind of girl I'd like to get to know better. Flash forward about a week, and we had found each other on Facebook and started talking every day. At first we just engaged in small talk: "How is your day going?" and "What's new?" and other kinds of questions that are normal when you just get to know someone. It wasn't long until she started to open up about some of the challenges she was having in her family. Soon she began to ask for help and advice. I didn't realize it at the time, but this was the start of my mission field. From that moment on, I met a lot of people at youth functions and events, occasionally in public, and over Facebook too. I added each of them to my mission field.

I am homeschooled, so I don't go to a public school campus everyday. In fact, it's rare that I go to a public school campus. Sometimes we homeschoolers go online to a "cyberschool" campus, while others of us use an offline curriculum. I've had both through the years, and both of them are nothing like a traditional campus. Unlike my friends at church, I don't have the "mission field" of a local high school or middle school in front of me all the time. But I still have a passion to share Jesus with everyone who needs Him. Since I don't have the opportunities for sharing Jesus like other Christian students do, I need to find other ways to share Jesus, and that means I need to develop my own mission field.

Today that mission field is bigger and better than I could've ever imagined. Through the help of the Holy Spirit, I've also left a very big impression in a lot of peoples lives, and helped quite a few people along the way. I have friends in my mission field from a few towns over, in other states, and even a buddy I know up in Canada. It's funny where my pursuit of sharing Jesus has taken me.

As a homeschooler trying to enter the campus mission field, it can be difficult. It can be hard to see yourself as a Campus Missionary when there isn't even a campus. It can seem challenging to share the Gospel if there isn't anyone around to share it with. But it's not impossible to be a Campus Missionary as a homeschooler. In fact, it really isn't hard at all. Any homeschool student can develop their own mission field, if they put their mind to it.

Be Social

The most important thing I've learned in my mission field is to be social. Get to know your neighborhood kids, make new friends at youth events, and generally look to connect with people wherever you go. Remember, if you don't have a campus, you have to create your mission field, and that means meeting people! If you want to be a homeschool Campus Missionary, you have to make sure you know people that you can spread the Gospel to. One important note: I encourage you to exercise caution. Not everyone you meet has good intentions or will consider you a friend, and you should talk with your parents about the people you meet.

Get Out There!

The big disadvantage of being a homeschooler is the lack of social interaction and the secluded environment, which is why you have to make an effort to meet new people. If you sit at home every day with little or no human contact other than your family, you probably won't have a very big mission field. Go outside, make some friends, and be involved. Then watch your mission field grow! I quickly learned getting out there was the key. Are there any homeschool groups in your area that meet together? Maybe that is a good place to start. Could you enroll in any of the local school sports activities or teams? When you go to different events with your church, be intentional to talk with people you meet and get to know them the best you can.

Start a Conversation, Start a Friendship

If you want to develop a mission field, you have to be willing to start a conversation. This can be challenging sometimes, especially for us homeschoolers, because as I mentioned above, we don't get a lot of social interaction compared to our public school peers. But realistically, you won't get to know anyone new or be able to add them to your mission field without starting a conversation. Introduce yourself, ask their name, and then ask them a question about themselves. Questions like, "What brings you here today?" and "What do you like to do for fun?" are great ways to get started.[1] As you get to know them, find out if you can friend them on social media. Find out what networks you both use (Instagram, Snapchat, Facebook, etc.), and then add them. Now they are a part of your mission field!

Stay Active

When I add someone to my mission field, it means I'm making a commitment to stay in touch with them over a longer period of time. And as a Campus Missionary, I am the one who has to take the initiative. In other words, I can't just add them to my social networks and expect them to start conversations with me. Instead, I have to start conversations with them. Sometimes it's as simple as asking how their week has been. At other times, it can be more intentional, like sharing a thought or a scripture verse from your devotional time, or from a sermon you enjoyed. Whatever you do, stay active and keep them engaged. Keep your mission field active!

Share Jesus

The more people I got to know and the more people I met, the more obvious it became that they needed someone to share the Gospel with them and help point them in the right direction. To be honest, I was really just trying to make new friends at first. But when I had started sharing Jesus, it just clicked in my head and I knew this was right.

Sometimes it seems like people are even more open to sharing their challenges and problems over the Internet than they are in person. This is one of the great advantages of being a homeschool Campus Missionary—everyone seems to have more courage behind the keyboard than they do face-to-face. They are bold with sharing their problems, but I am also bold in sharing Jesus with them. The Bible speaks directly to all kinds of challenges in life, and it can help with any situation you may encounter. So share the Word of God with your mission field, invite them to Jesus, and pray with them.

When I stared my mission, it was clear that a lot of people needed a lot of help. As time went on, I met more people with even more drastic problems. It escalated from family troubles and arguments, to depression, and even to drug use and worse. It wasn't pretty. It was clear to me what I needed to do. I had to show them the way to peace and hope and life by sharing Jesus with them.

Prepare Yourself for Rejection

One of the challenges of being homeschooled is not being used to the kinds of social ridicule our peers are accustomed to. Let's be honest, as homeschoolers we are very sheltered from a world that is, at times, very hard. And as great as it is to go through school on our own terms, the world is not getting any softer while we are in this shelter. Developing a mission field and sharing Jesus can open up great doors of opportunity for the Gospel, but it can also open up the doors for ridicule and criticism. And as homeschoolers, we are not always used to this kind of social treatment.

Not everyone will be so eager to hear about what you have to offer. Some will be open to Jesus and accept Him with open arms, glad to turn their lives over to God so He can help them with their troubles. Others will reject this idea entirely. In this life, and especially when preaching the Gospel, you will meet people that will laugh at you, mock you, and challenge your faith. You must stand firm, but not be judgmental, rude, or unkind. It's normal for people to disagree with you. And for anyone who doesn't follow Jesus with sincerity, it can be normal to become rude and angry, and even hostile when someone says something they don't agree with.

1 Timothy 4:12 says, "Do not let anyone look down on you because you are young, but set an example for the believers in speech, in conduct, in love, in faith, and in purity". When people reject your words about Jesus, and some people will, you have to brush it off and just keep trying. The most important thing to remember is that you can't force them into accepting Christ. You can lead them to the Cross, but you can't make them accept Jesus. They must make their own choices and decisions. If you press them into it, they will become even more reluctant, and you will lose any chance you had. Then you will have to start over with trying to lead them to God.

Plant, Water, and Let God Grow

If they do not accept Jesus, and do not want to become a Christian, that is okay (for now). Everyone plays a different role in leading a person to God. One person plants the seed, another person may water the seed, but God makes the seed grow.[2] Very rarely will one person plant, water, and harvest the seed of the Gospel, but it does happen every now and then. If a person doesn't want to become a Christian right away, or doesn't even want to accept that God exists, that is okay. Remember, you cannot pressure them into following God, anyway. What you can do is be there for them as a friend; keep them in your mission field. And when they need guidance from a trusted friend, you can take the opportunity to tell them how God is still there, and still wants to help them in their situation.

Look for Help When You Need To

I'm pretty young, but I've managed to build up a pretty good-sized mission field. It's so big that sometimes I don't know what to do, or how to answer, when a friend asks me a tough question, or has a really intense situation in their life. When I don't know what to say, I've always turned to my family, my pastors, or another trusted Christian leader to help me discover the right answers. They have never steered me wrong. Your pastors and parents always know best, so if you are having trouble, it's a great idea to let them know and ask for help.

Pray for Opportunities

This chapter is a basic guideline of what has worked for me, but I know it will not work for everyone. Your situation might be so unique that none of these things may apply, and that's fine. Begin to pray that the Holy Spirit would illuminate the path for you to share Jesus. It's important to find your own way to spread the Gospel, and to ask God to direct you. Although this book may be immensely helpful, it's always best to turn to God and let him lead you in the right direction. Whenever you get stuck, pray and seek out God's guidance. He may have something different planned. Sharing the Gospel is a great honor, one that can be difficult for homeschool kids. Remember to follow the guidance of the Holy Spirit. God has something great planned for you, and maybe this is where it all begins.

---

[1] A great book for learning how to start conversations is *Initiate: Powerful Conversations that Lead to Jesus*. It's available on Amazon.com, Kindle, and iBooks.
[2] 1 Corinthians 3:7-9.

ABOUT THE AUTHORS

Lee Rogers, General Editor and Lead Author

Lee is a husband to Christine and a father to Judah. He is the author of *Initiate: Powerful Conversations that Lead to Jesus*, and the lead author of *I Dare You: Spread the Gospel One Challenge at a Time*. A 20+ year veteran of Youth Ministry, Lee is a graduate of the University of Valley Forge, and holds a Doctorate of Ministry from Regent University.

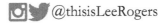 @thisisLeeRogers

CONTRIBUTING AUTHORS

Chance Abbott is the Youth Alive Missionary for South Texas. He is passionate about catalyzing a movement of students reaching students at school and beyond. He and his wife Katelyn have 3 children.

Tom Bachman is a veteran Youth Alive Missionary, serving faithfully in the state of Oregon for over 30 years. Tom loves to empower the local church to reach the 385,000 teenagers of Oregon. He is married to Dalleen, who serves the local community through nursing.

Aaron Benick was a Campus Missionary and a homeschooler. He helped pioneer Campus Missionary methods for non-traditional school students. He is active in his church and loves to create, whether by writing, making music, or anything else.

Sam Blevins earned his Bachelor's and Master's Degree in Music Education from Evangel University, and is an elementary music teacher in Colorado. He is husband to Allison and father to a growing family.

Joe Cali is the Youth Alive missionary for Pennsylvania and Delaware. An experienced youth pastor, Joe was active on the local high school campus through service and outreach. He and his wife Beckie have five children.

Dave Freeland is a church planter in North Carolina. He was previously the Youth Alive Missionary for Maryland, Virginia, and West Virginia. He is a graduate of Bethel College in Hampton, Virginia, and has a Master's degree from Liberty University. He and his wife Jillian have five kids.

Chris Gillott grew up in a ministry family, surrounded by music from his earliest memories. He and his wife Nia have two children, David Christopher and Evangelia Grace. When he gets his home and ministry work done he loves to go run.

John Ginnan, with his wife Caity, leads Youth Alive in the state of New York. He loves New York and enjoys journeying through it with his wife and two kids. John has served in youth ministry for nearly 20 years.

Ryan Goeden is a lover of Jesus, Joanna (wife), and Jack and Madeline (kids). He is the lead pastor of New Life Church in Springfield, MO, where he previously served as Student Ministries Pastor.

Kent Hulbert is a US/Youth Alive Missionary, coordinating Youth Alive nationally and serves on several national campus ministry and mission boards. He has been in Youth Ministry for more than 30 years. Kent's greatest joy is his family, including his wife Staci and their two grown children, Grant and Garrett.

Tristan Jepson is the Youth Alive Missionary for the state of Wyoming. She loves partnering with youth pastors and students to bring the hope of Jesus to school campuses. She is married to Rich and they have three children.

Bradly Keller has been working with students for over 20 years. He has worked with Young Life, Fellowship of Christian Athletes and now Youth Alive. His heart is to see students connect with Christ and share the hope of Christ with their friends.

Kami Kirschbaum was a Campus Missionary and Vo-Tech student near Pittsburgh. She is passionate about cutting hair, sharing Jesus with her friends and clients, and inviting them into the Body of Christ.

Anthony Lecocq serves the church in Baltimore, MD. He lives out loud as @anthonylecocq on way too many platforms, and at home with wife, Kandace, and son, Saja.

Kris Lewis served as the Youth Pastor with a passion to reach the unchurched students. He's married to his high school sweetheart, Danielle, and is a father to Londyn and Brittyn. He enjoys hunting, and science fiction.

Andy Lynn leads Youth Alive in New Jersey. A youth ministry veteran, Andy loves to help students with tools and community to actively grow and share their faith. He and his wife, Santina, have two beautiful daughters.

James Marti lives in Colorado Springs with his wife. He has four daughters, two son-in-laws and two grandchildren. He has been working with students for more than 30 years and is still passionate about seeing students become everything God has created and called them to be!

Arin Nicholson is the Youth Alive Missionary for the Potomac Ministry Network. Arin and his wife, Shauna, are passionate about equipping and encouraging students and leaders to share faith better. They are graduates of Southeastern University and have three children.

Peter and Joanna Reeves speak to audiences all over the United States. They are former Campus Missionaries who led Christian clubs during high school. They have a passion to see people experience and operate in the power of God.

Jessica Riner is the Youth Alive Missionary for Georgia. She is passionate about investing in the lives of students and seeing them grow to their full potential in Christ. She loves Jesus, her husband Ken, dark chocolate, peanut butter, and coffee.

Christine Rogers is a professional educator. She is a graduate of the University of Valley Forge, Penn State University, and has a Doctor of Education from the University of Florida. She and her husband, Lee, are kept busy by their son, Judah.

Forrest Rowell is a Rocky Mountain Youth Alive Missionary, where he serves churches in Colorado and Utah. He is a graduate of Southwestern University in Waxahachie, Texas. Forrest is married to Hannah and they have nine kids (a.k.a. "the mini mafia"): Rocco, Bruno, Simona, Francesca, Franco, Serafina, Leonardo, Massimo, and Filomena.

Ben Russell has served as Youth Alive Missionary in Alabama for over 10 years & has been in student ministries for 20+ years. He is a graduate of Southeastern University in Lakeland, Fl. He is married to Terra & has 2 kids - Knox & Anna.

Doug Sayers is a missionary and the former District Youth Director for the PennDel Ministry Network of the Assemblies of God. With more than three decades of Youth Ministry experience, Doug works to catalyze youth ministry globally. He is husband to Susan, and father to Chad and Jaclyn.

Linda Seiler is a Chi Alpha missionary and serves as the executive director for ReStory Ministries, a nonprofit established to equip ministry leaders on LGBTQ matters. Linda holds a PhD from the Assemblies of God Seminary, is an avid golfer, and is cat mom to feline Facebook sensations Bo & Tabby.

Wes Sheley pastors in Pendelton, Oregon and previously served as a Youth Alive Missionary in Oregon and Idaho. Wes is passionate about encouraging everyone to be a missionary to their sphere of influence.

George Volz is the youth pastor at Life Christian Fellowship in suburban Philadelphia. Jesus transformed his life in his early 20s, and now he is thrilled to use his passion and experience to solidify a life of purpose that will have eternal dividends.

Grayson Wade leads Youth Alive in the state of Arkansas. Grayson is passionate about reaching the lost and equipping students to share Jesus with their friends. He is married to Abigail, a middle school teacher, and they have two dogs.

Billy Willis and his wife, Katy, serve as the Youth Alive Missionaries in Illinois. Billy has over 15 years of youth ministry experience. He is the product of a church kid's invitation to youth group and is passionate about inspiring students to reach their peers with the Gospel.

Of all the challenges a Christian faces today, sharing the Faith with others can be one of the most intimidating. But it doesn't have to be! What if sharing the Gospel could occur naturally in a conversation about family, hobbies, or dreams?

Initiate: Powerful Conversations That Lead To Jesus
Lee Rogers

Anyone can learn to have powerful conversations, great relationships, and discover natural opportunities to share the Gospel in the process!

Available in print and eBook at www.initiateconversations.com, Amazon.com, Barnes & Noble, and iBooks.

Accompanying Sermons and Small Group Lessons also available at www.initiateconversations.com.

Made in the USA
Columbia, SC
06 October 2022

68870604R00164